CASES FOR ANALYSIS IN MARKETING

CASES FOR ANALYSIS IN MARKETING

W. Wayne Talarzyk

The Ohio State University

The Dryden Press
Hinsdale, Illinois

Editorial-Production Services Provided by
Cobb/Dunlop, Publisher Services, Inc.

DRYDEN PRESS PUBLICATIONS IN MARKETING

Principles of Marketing and Marketing Management

Louis E. Boone, *The University of Tulsa*
David L. Kurtz, *Eastern Michigan University*
CONTEMPORARY MARKETING, Second Edition (77)
FOUNDATIONS OF MARKETING (77)

Eugene M. Johnson, *University of Rhode Island*
Ray S. House, *Loyola College*
Carl D. McDaniel, Jr., *The University of Texas at Arlington*
READINGS IN CONTEMPORARY MARKETING, Second Edition (77)

Stephen K. Keiser, *University of Delaware*
Robert E. Stevens, *Oral Roberts University*
Lynn J. Loudenback, *Iowa State University*
STUDY GUIDE TO CONTEMPORARY MARKETING, Second Edition (77)

W. Wayne Talarzyk, *The Ohio State University*
CONTEMPORARY CASES IN MARKETING (74)
CASES FOR ANALYSIS IN MARKETING (77)

David T. Kollat
Roger D. Blackwell, *The Ohio State University*
James F. Robeson, *The Ohio State University*
STRATEGIC MARKETING (72)

Philip Kotler, *Northwestern University*
MARKETING DECISION MAKING: A MODEL BUILDING APPROACH (71)

Ronald R. Gist, *University of Denver*
MARKETING AND SOCIETY: TEXT AND CASES, Second Edition (74)
READINGS: MARKETING AND SOCIETY, Second Edition (74)

Vern Terpstra, *The University of Michigan*
INTERNATIONAL MARKETING (72)

Eberhard E. Scheuing, *St. John's University*
NEW PRODUCT MANAGEMENT (74)

Consumer Behavior and Marketing Research

James F. Engel, *Wheaton College*
David T. Kollat
Roger D. Blackwell, *The Ohio State University*
CONSUMER BEHAVIOR, Second Edition (73)
CASES IN CONSUMER BEHAVIOR (70)

Roger D. Blackwell, *The Ohio State University*
James F. Engel, *Wheaton College*
W. Wayne Talarzyk, *The Ohio State University*
CONTEMPORARY CASES IN CONSUMER BEHAVIOR (77)

Carl E. Block, *The University of Missouri at Columbia*
Kenneth J. Roering, *The University of Missouri at Columbia*
ESSENTIALS OF CONSUMER BEHAVIOR (76)

Gilbert A. Churchill, *The University of Wisconsin*
MARKETING RESEARCH: METHODOLOGICAL FOUNDATIONS (76)

Gerald Zaltman, *University of Pittsburgh*
Philip C. Burger, *SUNY at Binghamton*
MARKETING RESEARCH: FUNDAMENTALS AND DYNAMICS (75)

Randall L. Schultz, *Purdue University*
Gerald Zaltman, *University of Pittsburgh*
Philip C. Burger, *SUNY at Binghamton*
CASES IN MARKETING RESEARCH (75)

Franco M. Nicosia, *The University of California at Berkeley* (ed.)
Yoram Wind, *The Wharton School, University of Pennsylvania* (ed.)
BEHAVIORAL MODELS FOR MARKET ANALYSIS: FOUNDATIONS FOR
  MARKETING ACTION (77)

Gerald Zaltman, *The University of Pittsburgh*
Christian R. A. Pinson
Reinhard Angelmar, *Northwestern University*
METATHEORY AND CONSUMER RESEARCH (73)

Paul E. Green, *The Wharton School, University of Pennsylvania*
Vithala R. Rao, *Cornell University*
APPLIED MULTIDIMENSIONAL SCALING: A COMPARISON OF AP-
  PROACHES AND ALGORITHMS (72)

Paul E. Green, *The Wharton School, University of Pennsylvania*
Yoram Wind, *The Wharton School, University of Pennsylvania*
MULTIATTRIBUTE DECISIONS IN MARKETING: A MEASUREMENT AP-
  PROACH (73)

Retailing

Raymond A. Marquardt, *University of Wyoming*
James C. Makens, *University of Dallas*
Robert G. Roe, *University of Wyoming*
RETAIL MANAGEMENT: SATISFACTION OF CONSUMER NEEDS (75)

Advertising

S. Watson Dunn, *The University of Illinois*
Arnold M. Barban, *The University of Illinois*
ADVERTISING: ITS ROLE IN MODERN MARKETING, Third Edition (74)

PREFACE

An increasing number of instructors are searching for ways to make their introductory marketing courses a more meaningful learning experience for their students. Involved in this objective is the desire to make these courses more relevant by introducing students to real-life organizations and their marketing situations.

This book is designed to assist this group of instructors in reaching their objectives by providing a collection of contemporary marketing cases dealing with a wide range of marketing situations for varying types of firms and organizations. Issues for analysis run the gamut from broad strategy decisions to relatively specific problems involving one of the functions of marketing. Organizations range from some of the largest firms in the country down to one-person operations. A variety of products and services are represented, including fast foods, soft drinks, automobiles, computers, airlines, contraceptives, funeral services, banking, religion, and postal service.

Cases included in this text can be taught via the traditional approach to the case method involving identification of the problem, development of alternatives, analysis of alternatives, and specifying recommendations. Many instructors, however, may prefer to provide somewhat greater structure and direction for their students in terms of specific topics for analysis. To meet the needs of this group of instructors, a special series of self-contained analysis forms have been developed for each case.

These analysis forms, positioned in the back of the text, provide space for students to respond to specific questions about each case and carry out other activities associated with the analysis of the case. Each form is perforated for easy removal from the text for submission to the instructor for evaluation.

This text is designed to accompany either *Contemporary Marketing,* second edition, or *Foundations of Marketing,* both by Louis E. Boone and David L. Kurtz. It is, however, equally appropriate for use in conjunction with any other comprehensive introductory marketing text.

Organization of the text includes a series of introductory cases to provide an overview of marketing. The next five sections focus on specific marketing areas such as consumer behavior, product strategy, distribution strategy, promotional strategy, and pricing strategy. A separate section is included to present some of the emerging dimensions in the application of marketing principles. The concluding section provides a series of comprehensive cases designed to allow the student to synthesize his or her understanding of marketing.

As with any book of this type, many companies, organizations, and key executives must necessarily provide valuable assistance, information, and cooperation. These contributions are gratefully acknowledged in a special section of this text. It is appropriate here, however, to express sincere appreciation to a group of colleagues who provided insights, assurances, and evaluations at key points in the development of this book. Without holding them responsible for the end result, special thanks go to: Dale D. Achabal, Robert Bartels, Roger D. Blackwell, W. Arthur Cullman, Terry Deutscher, Dennis Garber, and James F. Robeson.

Columbus, Ohio   W. Wayne Talarzyk
February 1977

ACKNOWLEDGMENTS

A large number of individuals and organizations were very helpful in the successful completion of this collection of marketing cases for analysis. It is with much appreciation that all of these people and their organizations are acknowledged as having made valuable contributions to the development of this book.

Two professors willingly gave permission to have their original case manuscripts modified somewhat for inclusion in this text. Special appreciation goes to J. D. Claxton, University of British Columbia (Canadian Automobile Association) and Lionel A. Mitchell, Acadia University (Harper Bank). Jeffrey Eisenman was also very helpful in the development of several cases.

Appreciation is also expressed to the following individuals for their willingness to cooperate in the development of cases on firms and organizations with which they are associated:

Zelma Bishop
Joseph Block
Milton J. Bryson
Bob N. Daniel
John Diederich
William T. Fortner
David T. Girves
Ben F. Goldsmith

Frank Hewens
R. C. Hockney
Eleanor Jacobs
Emily Leonard
John L. Lowden
Fred Poppe
Ralph Rickett
Pete Rogers

Joseph Serian
Heather S. Sturt
Joseph A. Sugarman
Charles Tuller
Nancy E. Vaughan
Stephen J. Waling
Graydon D. Webb

CONTENTS

PART SEVEN

Emerging Dimensions   115

PART EIGHT

Comprehensive Cases   133

CASES FOR ANALYSIS IN MARKETING

PART ONE
INTRODUCTORY CASES

CASE 1

WENDY'S INTERNATIONAL, INC. (A)

WENDY'S OLD FASHIONED HAMBURGERS

Since 1969 the emergence of Wendy's Old Fashioned Hamburgers as an addition to the way of life in communities across the United States and Canada has provided the food service industry with one of its most exciting chapters. As of December 31, 1975, there were 252 restaurants open in the United States and Canada, with an additional 72 units under construction. By the end of 1976, the firm anticipates serving customers from Wendy's locations in over 200 cities in more than 33 states.

Company Background

Wendy's was founded by R. David Thomas who was previously associated with Kentucky Fried Chicken and Arthur Treacher's Fish and Chips. Thomas presently serves as Chairman and Chief Executive Officer. Robert L. Barney, presently President and Chief Operating Officer, joined Wendy's in 1970. He started in the fast food business in 1962 when he became an owner of a Kentucky Fried Chicken franchise, later becoming a regional Vice-President in charge of 135 stores. For a short period of time before joining Wendy's he was Vice-President of Operations at Arthur Treacher's Fish and Chips.

Much of Wendy's recent growth has come from rapid expansion of the franchise system. At the end of 1975, Wendy's had 183 franchised units in operation, compared with 51 at the end of 1974. Franchises are assigned for twenty years on an area basis. The cost for a franchise is $10,000 per unit with a continuing 4 percent of sales service fee paid monthly to the parent company. Most of Wendy's franchises are owned by experienced operators who have had previous experience in the food service field.

Wendy's is also directing considerable attention toward expanding company-owned outlets. This is being accomplished in two ways—either by buying back existing franchises or by constructing its own company-owned units. To date, management has not opened a unit which they subsequently had to close down.

The typical Wendy's building is about 30 × 70 feet, seats 80 to 100 people, and has a parking area for 30 to 45 cars. Most units are built on a ½- to ¾-acre lot as opposed to a typical McDonald's or Burger King which usually occupy an acre or more. The basic reason that Wendy's needs less land than the other two operations is that a drive-in window accounts for 35 to 40 percent of a unit's total sales. Those customers who use the pick-up window obviously do not require parking spaces or inside eating areas. Exhibit 1.1 shows pictures of a typical Wendy's unit.

An average investment of $285,000 is required to construct a Wendy's unit. Of this total about 38 percent goes for the building, another 38 percent for real estate, and the remaining 24 percent for equipment. The typical Wendy's outlet averages about $525,000 in annual sales.

Product Offering

Wendy's places primary emphasis upon consistent quality in all areas of food preparation and presentation. The firm uses 100 percent pure beef which is delivered in bulk and pattied fresh every morning in each of its restaurants. The patties are cooked slowly to retain their natural juices and flavors. Whether the customer orders the quarter-pound single (69 cents), the half-pound double ($1.25), or the three-quarter triple ($1.75) the hamburger is served directly from the grill. By mixing and matching the eight available condiments, a Wendy's customer can specify one of 256 different ways to have his or her hamburger served. Current sales break down into approximately 70 percent singles, 25 percent doubles, and 5 percent triples.

Chili is also on the menu at 69 cents. In addition to being desired by customers this product serves a unique secondary purpose. To keep the hamburgers fresh for customers no cooked patties are kept on the grill for more than four minutes. In order to eliminate this potential meat waste factor, hamburgers not served within the four-minute time period are steamed in a kettle and used for the next day's chili.

French fries, Frostys, coffee, tea, milk, and soft drinks round out the complete menu, Frosty, a Wendy's exclusive, is a thick, creamy blend of chocolate and vanilla (much like a very thick milkshake) served with a spoon. An illustration of Wendy's product mix is shown in Exhibit 1.2.

Communication with Consumers

A great obstacle facing Wendy's in any new market is that the consumer is likely to view it as another McDonald's, Burger King, or Burger Chef. As a result it is necessary for Wendy's to educate the consumer as to how and why it is different than other hamburger restaurants. The following four points outline the areas in which Wendy's management perceives the firm to be different from its competition:

1. Wendy's hamburgers are made the "Old Fashioned" way with fresh beef that is never frozen. They are cooked slowly on the grill and prepared to the customer's order with an unlimited choice of condiments. In addition, each sandwich is served on a warm bun. Sandwiches are never cooked or wrapped ahead of time. They are served directly from the grill.
2. Wendy's provides the ultimate in take-home food convenience by providing the customer with Pick-Up Window service. While others may have a drive-thru window, none can provide the speed of service and consistent high-quality product that Wendy's is famous for. This adds up to a big benefit to the consumer, namely, fast, high-quality stay-in-the-car service.
3. Wendy's offers a full menu of top quality products. The chili is made fresh every day with almost a quarter pound of beef in each serving. Wendy's offers a consistently crisp and golden french fry that is served moments from the fryer. Wendy's has an all-natural dairy product dessert, the "Frosty." It's cool and creamy with a rich chocolate/vanilla flavor that's better than ice cream. And it's so thick you have to eat it with a spoon.
4. Finally, Wendy's offers a family dining room that's warm, inviting, bright, and cheerful. The turn-of-the-century decor includes Tiffany lamps, Victorian parlor beads, bentwood chairs, and table tops printed with turn-of-the-century advertisements. Additional touches of wood paneled walls, colorful carpeting, and low music completes the setting.

Each Wendy's outlet spends at least 4 percent of sales on advertising.

Media used to communicate with the consumer include newspapers, television, radio, billboards, bus cards, and taxi tops. Exhibit 1.3 shows examples of some of the advertisements used in print media. Typical television and radio commercials focus on similar themes.

EXHIBIT 1.1
Pictures of a Typical Wendy's Restaurant

EXHIBIT 1.2
Wendy's Product Offering

EXHIBIT 1.3
Examples of Typical Print Advertisements for Wendy's

CASE 2

PEPSI-COLA COMPANY
THE PEPSI CHALLENGE

On July 12, 1976, Pepsi-Cola Company placed a full-page advertisement in the *New York Times* which said in part:

> We have believed for a long time that we produce a better-tasting product than our leading competitor. But we wanted to be sure of that fact. We did not want to advertise it until we had it documented by careful, objective, independent research. We now have that documentation. *Truth in advertising is very important to us. And the truth is: nationwide, more Coca-Cola drinkers prefer Pepsi than Coke.*

Situational Development

Dallas had historically been a very poor market for Pepsi-Cola. Coca-Cola had held about 27 percent of the Dallas market with Dr Pepper (home offices in Dallas) in second place with 23 percent. Pepsi-Cola ranked a distant third with an 8 percent of the market compared with its national market share of 17 percent.

In early 1975 Pepsi-Cola decided it was time to do something about its meager share of the Dallas area soft drink market. Research had shown that Dallas consumers almost always *believed* they could tell the difference between the taste of Coke and the taste of Pepsi and that they preferred the taste of Coke. Pepsi-Cola marketing people, however, believed that the problem was that most Coke drinkers had never tasted Pepsi.

An independent research firm was retained to conduct blind taste tests to find out which taste Coke consumers really preferred. Results indicated that more than half the Coca-Cola drinkers tested actually preferred the taste of Pepsi.

The research was soon translated into a local advertising campaign called "The Pepsi Challenge." Using a hidden camera to photograph local consumers taking the blind taste test, television commercials claimed: "More than half the Coca-Cola drinkers tested in the Dallas-Fort Worth area prefer the taste of Pepsi-Cola."

Sales of Pepsi-Cola began to increase in Dallas immediately and a variety of responses began to develop. These activities, as viewed from Pepsi-Cola's perspective, are chronicled in the news release in Exhibit 2.1.

Within a year Pepsi-Cola's share of the Dallas market had increased 50 percent, although most of the increase apparently came at the expense of cheaper, little-known brands. In addition, evaluation of the effectiveness of the taste comparison advertising campaign was made difficult because of the price cutting promotion going on simultaneously by both sides.

National Research Results

Based on the experience in Dallas and other local areas and the activities of Coca-Cola, Pepsi-Cola's decided to commission a national study comparing the taste preferences of the two brands. Motivational Programmers, Inc. (MPI) of New York, an independent marketing research company, conducted the research.

The research methodology involved a weighted national probability sample of over 3,000 males and females fourteen years of age and over. At no time were the brands identified to the respondent before the taste test was completed. Opaque insulated bags were used to bring the products into the respondents' homes.

After being poured into clear plastic glasses behind an 18 × 24-inch screen, one of the brands was placed in the respondent's right hand and the other in his or her left hand. The interview form indicated which hand would be used for the respective brands so that neither would always be "left" or "right." In addition, Pepsi was tasted first in one-half the tests, while Coke was tasted first in the other half.

Before tasting each product, respondents were asked to sip water to clear their palate. Ice was not used in the already chilled product so that it would not be diluted to any degree whatever.

After tasting both brands, respondents were asked: "Now, thinking about the two colas—all things considered, which of the two did you like better, the one in your right hand or the one in your left?" The results of the study are given in Exhibit 2.2.

Concluding Comments

At the news conference announcing the results of the national taste test, Victor A. Bonomo, President of Pepsi-Cola Company, stated, "I emphasize that even though we now have the research available that will allow us to introduce the Challenge anywhere, at any time, we will use prudent judgment in doing so; 'The Pepsi Challenge' is still a local advertising campaign designed for specific and selected markets. Our commercials are straightforward, based on objective and clear research. We are not trying to mislead or confuse the consumer. The tag line of all Pepsi Challenge commercials sums up the key message: 'Take the Pepsi Challenge, Let *Your* Taste Decide.' " A sample advertisement for the Pepsi Challenge is shown in Exhibit 2.3.

EXHIBIT 2.1
Pepsi-Cola Company's News Release on the Pepsi Challenge (July 6, 1976)

THE PEPSI CHALLENGE
What Are the Issues?

More Than Half the Coca-Cola Drinkers Tested Actually Preferred Pepsi.

We first found it out in Dallas, Texas, where Coke outsold Pepsi 3 to 1. We conducted side-by-side *blind* taste tests between Pepsi and Coca-Cola. The bottles were hidden and the products were in drinking glasses identified only as "M" and "Q." The people tested were dyed-in-the-wool Coca-Cola drinkers. The results were amazing and clear-cut. More than half the Coca-Cola drinkers tested in Dallas/Fort Worth preferred the taste of Pepsi.

What Was Coca-Cola's First Response?

The Coca-Cola Company's first response to this was to do local commercials with Coca-Cola drinkers tasting both products in a side-by-side test with each product identified. Naturally, people picked the one they normally drink. Coke's claim: Coke outsells Pepsi in Dallas. Needless to say, we knew that already. Also, Coke wasn't responsive to the issue: which tastes better, Pepsi or Coke? We did not consider it a very good answer to the Pepsi Challenge.

What Happened Then?

We continued the Pepsi Challenge in Dallas to the point where our sales increases amazed even ourselves.

What Was Coca-Cola's Next Response?

Our competitor's response to this was to do a national campaign wherein blindfolded people were asked to decide which they liked better, Fresca or Pepsi. Even though two-thirds of the participants in this strange test of "apples" and "oranges" chose Pepsi-Cola, the competition seemed to think this was an effective answer to the Pepsi Challenge.

And Then What Happened?

We took the Pepsi Challenge to other Texas cities: Corpus Christi and San Antonio. Again and again Pepsi won. More than half the Coca-Cola drinkers tested preferred the taste of Pepsi.

Then What Did Coke Do?

They compared apples to oranges again. Coca-Cola responded with a campaign comparing the calories in Tab, a one-calorie diet drink to those of our new product, Pepsi Light, a reduced-calorie lemony cola. Needless to say, they carefully avoided comparing one-calorie Tab to one-calorie Diet Pepsi. This could not honestly be considered an answer to the Pepsi Challenge.

What Did Pepsi Do?

We took the Challenge to Detroit, Flint, and Grand Rapids. Again and again, Pepsi won. More than half the Coca-Cola drinkers tested preferred the taste of Pepsi.

What Did Coke Do?

Coke ran a commercial in Dallas, suggesting that Pepsi was winning only because people liked the letter "M" better than the letter "Q." In the blindfold test "M" was the symbol for Pepsi, "Q" for Coke. Of course, unfortunately for Coke, this is nonsense; Dallas was the only city in which we used the letters "M" and "Q." In all other cities, we got the same results. We used "L" and "S." Pepsi won. We used different combinations of letters. Pepsi won. We used no letters. Pepsi won.

Now What Is Coke Up To?

Recently, in a number of markets like New York, Coke has begun a campaign in which they point out that Coke outsells Pepsi locally (they use the word "prefer"). Of course, they neglect to mention that this claim has nothing to do with taste. As in Dallas, their commercials show confirmed Coke drinkers reinforcing their own beliefs. Also, they neglect to point out that nationally when consumers do have a freedom of choice (as in food stores), Pepsi has outsold Coke for more than a year.

EXHIBIT 2.2
Results of Blind Taste Test Preference Between Pepsi-Cola and Coca-Cola

| | TOTAL SAMPLE | REGULAR DRINKERS OF | | |
		ANY CARBONATED SOFT DRINK	COCA-COLA	PEPSI-COLA
Prefer Pepsi-Cola	51.7%	52.6%	49.8%	58.2%
Prefer Coca-Cola	41.7	41.7	44.2	37.3
No Preference	6.6	5.7	6.0	4.5
	—	—	—	—
Total	100%	100%	100%	100%

EXHIBIT 2.3
Sample Print Advertisement for the Pepsi Challenge

"PEPSI-COLA" AND "PEPSI" ARE REGISTERED TRADEMARKS OF PepsiCo, INC.   "COCA-COLA" AND "COKE" ARE REGISTERED TRADEMARKS OF THE COCA-COLA COMPANY

Take the
Pepsi Challenge.
Let your taste decide.

Pepsi-Cola's blind taste test.
Maybe you've seen "The Pepsi Challenge" on TV.
It's a simple, straightforward taste test where Coca-Cola
drinkers taste Coca-Cola and Pepsi
without knowing which is which.
Then we ask them which one they prefer.

**More than half the
Coca-Cola drinkers
tested in Michigan
preferred Pepsi.**
Hundreds of Coca-Cola
drinkers from Michigan were
tested and we found that
more than half the people
tested preferred the taste
of Pepsi.

Let your taste decide.
We're not asking you to take our word for it. Or anyone
else's. Just try it yourself. Take The Pepsi Challenge
and let your taste decide.

BOTTLED BY (NAME AND ADDRESS OF BOTTLER GO HERE) UNDER APPOINTMENT FROM PepsiCo, INC., PURCHASE, N.Y.

CASE 3

HARPER BANK[1]
IMPLEMENTING THE MARKETING CONCEPT

In early 1969 top management of Harper Bank was considering the failure of the introduction of the marketing concept in banking. Some members of management who had heard of excellent results from the introduction of the marketing concept in goods-producing firms were beginning to wonder whether different conditions were not required for the successful implementation of the marketing concept in the banking business. Harper Bank management began a self-analysis to determine where the bank went wrong and what could and should be done at this stage.

In 1968 Harper Bank was faced with the challenge of increasing competition from the other chartered banks and a dynamic thrust by the trust companies in the financial services market. A few of Harper's top executives who had come into contact with some marketing professors at a business conference were impressed with what they heard about the advantages of the marketing concept and brought back the idea to the bank.

They thought if they were the first to truly introduce the marketing

[1]Modified for inclusion in this text with the permission of Lionel A. Mitchell, Acadia University, Wolfville, Nova Scotia, author of the original case.

concept into banking in Canada, with the changes in the Bank Act (The Revised Bank Act) which were introduced last year they should be able to anticipate and solve most of the problems which were likely to come to the fore—problems of customers and customers' demands and servicing, and problems arising out of the growth in foreign currency deposits, loans, and real estate management. The top executives thought they could introduce the change on a test or experimental basis in a few of their branches in Montreal.

Situational Information

Harper was one of Canada's leading chartered banks with head office in Montreal and branches throughout Canada and in many parts of the world. Most policy matters were initiated at head office; however, other matters were dealt with by divisional offices in the area where they arose. Divisional offices were located in Toronto, Winnipeg, Quebec City, Halifax, Edmonton, and Vancouver. Each divisional vice-president had a lending limit of $½ million, with any loan exceeding this limit requiring the approval of the board of directors at head office.

Harper Bank was established more than a century ago and expanded through internal growth and mergers. Its growth was considered fairly substantial up to 1946 but even more so from 1946 to the mid-sixties when the number of branches tripled and profit growth, assets, and foreign currency holdings more than doubled. The bank's main emphasis and target market were big business and large accounts. Not very much attention was given to wooing the small depositors and investors.

However, a wind of change was now about to be blown across the banking business and Harper predicted a struggle with its competitors to maintain their market share and perhaps to continue expansion of their operations. Management believed that a change in the bank's image and outlook was required. They thought a change in attitudes and approach was needed to cash in on increasing incomes and to stem the tide of greater and more intense competition from other banks and financial institutions. Moreover, they thought they would have to overcome the distorted and misunderstood image held by desired customers.

Initial "Marketing" Activities

In the late 1940's Harper Bank began to work on the idea of public relations, advertising, and other promotion and within ten years they had established a separate Public Relations and Advertising Department, headed by a manager who reported to the Secretary. This department supplied ink blotters and book covers for students, posters which were displayed at branches, bus and train advertising cards, small informative folders for branch disposal, and many other similar items too numerous to mention.

The common characteristic of each of these items was a message from Harper Bank; for instance, a message with descriptive pictures telling of the advantages of a savings account or a safety deposit box. This type of promotion may have been adequate for the period during which it was used, but the bank now found that it had to do much more. This led to more intensive promotional activities, such as the establishment of student tours, sponsoring of prizes at regional fairs and exhibitions, student scholarships, and display booths at industrial fairs. Banking had become more complex and competitive, and the bank was outgrowing its Public Relations and Advertising Department. It was time for a change.

Implementing Change

The responsibility for change would be placed in the marketing department under the marketing concept, the executives thought, if they understood the professors correctly. Consequently, a reorganization would have to take place. The Public Relations and Advertising Department could be enlarged into a marketing department with clearly defined functions left for the department to undertake.

The new marketing department under John Morgan, Assistant General Manager of Marketing, who came to Harper from the marketing department of a leading Canadian goods-manufacturing firm, set as objectives a major reorganization campaign designed to upgrade and modernize all services, to handle customers' services more effectively and efficiently, and to listen to and act upon customers' suggestions and complaints. John Morgan reported directly to Fred McKenzie, General Manager, who indicated to Morgan that he was in complete charge of the department and had "full rein" to implement any new marketing feature.

The reorganization had caused a change in the organizational structure of the bank at this particular branch. The bank had considered that a reorganization in structure, strategy, and operation was essential to profitably take advantage of the findings of the Royal Commission on Banking and Finance reflected in the 1967 revision of the Bank Act to encourage the development of a fully competitive financial system.

The Public Relations and Advertising Department was to be subordinated to the new Marketing Department and in time completely absorbed by it. One of the first projects of the Marketing Department was the redesign of banking forms using the new bank ensign and maroon and gold color. The uniforms and outfits of porters, messengers, pages, chauffeurs, and mail and service staff were redesigned to reflect the new bank image. Banking hours were to be extended for customer convenience. It was suggested that marketing departments be established at divisional offices in Quebec City, Montreal, Halifax, Toronto, Winnipeg, Edmonton, and Vancouver.

The Impact of Change

Within six months from its inception the Marketing Department's staff numbered 29. Most of the projects had been initiated, the Public Relations and Advertising Department was almost completely absorbed, that is, most of the duties were now performed by the Marketing Department, and extensive research had been in progress with a view to implementing marketing departments in the other regions.

About this time, however, problems began to arise and conflicts developed. Doubts were raised about the many and frequent changes. Many of the changes did not transpire as well as the bank had expected. Mr. Morgan, who was inexperienced in banking matters, had plunged into his job of introducing a marketing orientation with little or no cooperation and assistance from the old staff members, that is, the experienced bank personnel. Morgan relied entirely on his previous marketing knowledge and experience, but some of his ideas were considered unorthodox by the banking public as well as many of the staff, including his subordinates and his superiors. Morgan secretly admitted that he did not care what the staff thought of the new concept; it was a good thing and it would be implemented.

In the meantime, there was a clash with McKenzie and in the weeks that followed Morgan was unable to patch this relationship, which eventually led to his dismissal. A new Public Relations and Advertising Department was set up to perform the marketing function and Peter Forrest was installed as manager of the department.

CASE 4

HONEYWELL
FIRE AND SMOKE DETECTOR

Today, the importance of early fire detection and warning is getting attention as never before. Throughout the nation, new legislation has been making fire and smoke alarms mandatory in more and more types of residences. In addition, government and private-agency programs are being released to educate the public on the need for protecting lives against fire. Among these educational activities are special projects by the National Fire Protection and Control Administration and by the National Fire Protection Association.

Honeywell, a major producer of control devices for the home, has developed a dual-chamber ionization detector which has the capability of detecting minute particles of combustion at the earliest (or incipient) stages of a fire. As a result, it can detect the beginning of a fire before the smoke, flame, and heat create serious hazards and panic.

Importance of Early Detection
Over 300,000 Americans are injured by fire each year and over 12,000 lives are lost. These statistics place the United States' hazard of death loss by fire

at nearly twice that of any other nation. The U.S. Children's Bureau lists fire as one of the three major causes of premature death among children one to nine years old. Fire takes more lives in the one to four age group than any other cause except motor vehicle accidents.

Most fatal fires occur at night with little advance warning for the occupants to allow time for evacuation. Undiscovered fires produce smoke and fumes which seriously reduce the chances for successful evacuation. Since every moment counts, early warning is generally agreed to be the most important factor in saving lives and preventing personal injury from fire. It is estimated that only about 2 or 3 percent of the dwellings in the United States have early warning fire detection systems.

Honeywell's Expertise

Five years of intensive research and actual field experience on early warning needs, detection methods, and performance reliability went into the design of the Honeywell smoke detector. The dual-chamber ionization principle used in Honeywell's residential smoke detector is the same type as that used in the firm's fire protection and prevention systems installed in commercial and industrial buildings throughout the world.

Since 1885, Honeywell has manufactured a wide range of quality control devices for the home. This equipment includes such items as thermostats, gas, oil, and electric heating controls, air conditioning controls, water heater controls, humidity controls, and electronic air cleaners.

Product Description

All fires emit tiny combustion particles, some of which are visible while others are not. Both of the major types of detectors sold today—ionization and photocell—work by sounding an alarm when those particles are present. The basic difference, however, is that photocell detectors react only to visible particles while ionization type detectors are also activated by the invisible particles. Exhibit 4.1 shows the four stages of a fire and where various types of detectors are activated.

Honeywell's detector, like other ionization types, has a special chamber where the surrounding air is continuously sampled. When combustion particles, either visible or invisible, enter the chamber, an 85-decibel alarm horn is activated. The dual-chamber design provides the benefit of automatically compensating the system for changes in temperature, pressure, and humidity. This feature makes possible maximum sensitivity for early fire warning and yet is not upset by normal changes in local environmental conditions. False alarms, therefore, are held to a minimum. The sensitivity setting can be changed to allow for special conditions of a location.

Because alarm maintenance is often neglected, the Honeywell detector is designed to operate with a minimum of attention. There are no batteries or bulbs to weaken or fail and no filters to clog. The solid-state design requires minimal attention (only an occasional vacuuming). As an additional assurance, a solid-state power indicator light lets the consumer know that the detector is in operation.

Other features of Honeywell's detector is that it can be mounted on the wall or ceiling on a standard electrical outlet box to minimize installation costs. For plug-in installations a snap-on electrical cord is available. A universally acceptable round cover is supplied with all models to better harmonize with the decor of consumers' homes.

Promotional Activities

Honeywell's packaging for its detectors provides an ideal point-of-purchase information base. Each package features dramatic full-color photos and gives passing shoppers details about the product's function. How-to photographs demonstrate simple installation procedures (permanent and plug-in) while the package bottom offers advice for smoke detector location within the home and other areas. A sturdy, vacuum-formed plastic display (detector included) is available to retailers with a minimum order of 48 retail-packaged detectors. It features a built-in test button that gives shoppers a startling demonstration of the product's 85-decibel alarm horn.

Retailers are also offered other sales support materials such as a variety of types of full-color sales literature, advertising materials for radio, television, and print media, and inserts to be enclosed with regular billings. Exhibits 4.2, 4.3, and 4.4 are illustrative of this type of support. A cooperative advertising plan for reimbursement of local advertising costs up to a maximum available allowance of $2.00 per unit purchase is also available.

EXHIBIT 4.1
Stages of a Fire and Types of Detection

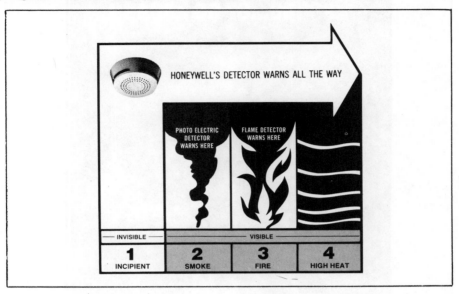

EXHIBIT 4.2
Sample of Item to Be Used as Billing Enclosure or Hand-out

EXHIBIT 4.3
Example of Print Advertisement for Honeywell's Detector

It doesn't wait for smoke or flames to wake you up.

This is the new Honeywell Fire and Smoke Detector. It can smell fire before visible smoke or flames erupt.

That can give you and your family precious extra time to escape, especially if fire strikes while you sleep.

It takes smoke, flames or heat to set off some home fire alarms. The Honeywell alarm has a dual chamber ionization sensor, which can detect fire in its earliest, incipient stage.

This stage can last for minutes, or only seconds. No smoke and flames are present. But invisible particles of combustion are.

The Honeywell Fire and Smoke Detector senses these particles. And sounds a prolonged, piercing alarm to awaken everyone in your home.

Cost? Under $40. Installation? Simple. Just hang it up and plug it in. Or wire it permanently. Either way, no batteries to fail or replace.

In case of fire, the Honeywell Fire and Smoke Detector won't wait for smoke or flames to wake you up. So don't delay. Buy one (or as many as your home needs) today.

Protect your family tonight.

Honeywell

Fire & Smoke Detector

It smells fire before visible smoke or flames break out.

23

EXHIBIT 4.4
Television Storyboard for Honeywell's Detector

Campbell-Mithun, Inc. ADVERTISING
Northstar Center / Minneapolis, Minnesota 55402 / Tel. 800-7000

CLIENT: Honeywell/Residential
PRODUCT:
CODE NO./TITLE: QHBI7601/"Fire and Smoke Detector"
JOB NO.: 6-119-200   DATE: February, 1976   LENGTH: :30 T/C

1. (Natural sfx under, Anncr VO) When fire strikes your home, time is critical.

2. A few extra seconds of early warning can make the difference between e...p ...

3. ...or no escape.

4. But the...

5. ...Honeywell Fire and Smoke Detector...

6. ...can smell fire before there is visible smoke or flame.

7. And that buys time...

8. ...(Buzzzzzz)...a few extra seconds that can save your family's lives.

9. So buy the...

10. ...Honeywell Fire and Smoke Detector.

11. Just hang it up...plug it in... and buy a few precious seconds more.

12. (Sfx: siren)

PART TWO

CONSUMER BEHAVIOR

CASE 5

TULLER FRUIT FARM (A)[1]
ROADSIDE MARKETING

My wife and I started in the marketing business (about sixteen years ago) from a picnic table, like most of you. You know what happens when you start feeding people: They come back if you have quality merchandise (and we felt we did). When we started we had a peach orchard. It was a beautiful thing. We had 10 acres and made about $4,000 on it. Since then, we've had one crop in ten years; frost and winter freezes kill them every year.

So, we went into the apple business. We have 14 acres of apples now, and it has been a real hassle getting them picked (as you all know, labor today is about as wishy-washy as it can get). At the present time we are thinking about taking half of it out and growing more sweet corn. We started about three years ago with 8 acres of sweet corn; we are now raising 90 acres of corn. Last year we sold 40,000 dozen, retail.

To get back to when we started, we left our picnic table and went to our garage; sold out of it two or three years. Then, about five years ago, we

[1]Adapted from a talk given by Charles Tuller at the Fourteenth Annual Ohio Roadside Marketing Conference, January 6–8, 1974, sponsored by the Department of Agricultural Economics and Rural Sociology, The Ohio State University, and The Ohio Cooperative Extension Service.

built a salesroom. (See Exhibit 5.1.) It is not too colorful, red and white, but there is a little room (16 feet wide by about 24 feet long) on one side and more action goes on in that room than any place we have ever had. It is known as the Donut Shop.

Product/Service Offerings

I don't know if any of you are familiar with it or not, but we've really got a tiger by the tail. Three years ago we started out in the donut business, and (the 1st of October) our grand total sales in donuts for the day was $8. On a Saturday this fall we sold $1,600 worth of donuts—that is, 1,200 dozen. We started at 2:30 in the morning and quit at 8:00 at night, and I want to tell you that it is really a rat race. This past year we ran 150,000 dozen in sales.

I'd like to give you a little advice from personal experience. Donuts are a good money maker (about 40 percent profit on your product) but it is a hassle. Everybody can't roll dough and you have to know what to do with it after you have it rolled out. When you put yeast into warm water with flour in it, you can't walk out the door and say "Well, I'll be back in an hour," because let me tell you, that stuff grows.

We have one of those peanut butter machines downstairs; it is great. You start that thing up (of course, the one we have makes so much noise it sounds like it is going to die) and it jumps up and down on the counter. The peanuts get stuck and you have to use a screwdriver to get them out, but the customer likes that. If it's too slick, he won't buy anymore. It was nothing for us to go through 90 pounds of peanuts on a Saturday; we have gone through as much as 125 pounds. That old thing really goes. It is a good machine and works well, but I don't know whether you buy or lease them now. We sell close to 2 tons of peanut butter a year.

Cider is another thing. We started off with a little cider press about five years ago and that first year we pressed 5,000 gallons. The second year it was 10,000; third year 20,000; and last year it was 30,000 gallons. I'll tell you, it keeps one awfully busy. I'd like to invite all of you to come up and see what we've got. It is not the world's greatest press, but the way I have it set up is a one-man operation. If you are like me, you don't like other ding-a-lings in the background. (My wife says if I could put a motor on my hind end I could go a lot faster!) Anyway, I have six motors working the press, and we can make about 1,500 gallons a day (which is pretty good for one man). Of course, my dad bottles it all—that helps.

Promotional Considerations

We do a lot of tours, from September to November. We have a special lady we hire to come in and give a guided tour through our orchard, our packing house, and through the cider operation. On the tour, we give them all the cider they want and, if we've got any unfortunate donuts left over, they get them too. It works out really good. We had about 3,500 kids come through last year. If you want a real rat race, invite 3,500 kids through your place; they can be everywhere you don't think they are going to be.

Some people may not understand this, but I don't advertise. I used to, but not any more because we feel that our action is the key now. You have to advertise at the start, but not after you get your clientele and you are established.

Overall Operating Philosophy

I feel—and I am sure my wife will agree—that the decor of the building adds to sales. I don't care what anybody tells you, if you've got atmosphere you will sell it. Ours is an old country store. Everything in it (and the people too, I think) is old fashioned—fixtures, antiques, clocks, etc. We keep two fires going in Franklin stoves, one at either end of the room.

Now we are only open Monday through Saturday. I can't take another day, so we close on Sunday (that is family day for us). We are open 7 A.M. to 6 P.M., including Saturday; we started out 7 A.M. to 9 P.M. We are making the same amount of money as we did when we had longer hours, but the wife and I communicate more and have more fun together with the kids. We weren't sure if it was going to work, but it really does. For those of you who are wondering if closing on Sunday will work for you or whether it won't, I'll guarantee you won't lose $50 a week—if you really want to keep track of it. You may not lose anything. We feel we lose nothing, plus have more time with the kids. You know, once they are sixteen, they are up and gone.

By the way, anything you can do (I don't care what it is—if it is just cleaning light bulbs), *do it* when customers are in the building. You will sell more. If we are making donuts frantically, we sell more than if we have a bunch sitting there for everybody to buy. If a butcher is cutting meat, a customer will buy what he is cutting, not that thing laying there in the case. He wants the fresh cut. The same with donuts, apples, peanut butter—you name it. The action is what they like, and I think that is the key.

EXHIBIT 5.1
Photograph of Tuller Fruit Farm

Photograph courtesy of Ralph Rickett Photography.

30

CASE 6

CANADIAN AUTOMOBILE ASSOCIATION[1]

RESEARCHING CONSUMER BEHAVIOR

In the fall of 1971 the Essex County Club (ECC), the Windsor affiliate of Canadian Automobile Association (CAA), was interested in evaluating their driver services. Mr. Denis Savoie, Director of Public Relations, had read of other automobile associations having research done by university students. Thus, he contacted the local business faculty to see if some sort of survey for the ECC could be done as a graduate student project.

Background
The Canadian Automobile Association was established in 1912 and by 1971 it had 64 branches across Canada. The association was best known for its emergency road service. If members had car trouble (such as car will not start, out of gas, or flat tire), they could call one of the 25,000 affiliated service stations and get assistance free of charge. Many additional services were also available to members such as travel publications, travel agency, automobile touring information, certain types of insurance, and others.

[1]Modified for inclusion in this text with the permission of John D. Claxton, University of British Columbia. The original case was prepared by Linday Kwai-Pun under the direction of Professor Claxton.

Membership in the CAA was open to anyone holding a driver's license. Two types of membership were offered, master and associate. The first family member to become a member joined as a master member, and paid 20 dollars per year (plus an administration fee of 5 dollars in the first year). A master membership entitled only one person to CAA services. For example, if the husband was a master member, the wife could not get CAA assistance unless she also was a member. Additional family members could join as associate members for 15 dollars per year.

CAA in Southwestern Ontario

The head office of the CAA in southwestern Ontario was the Essex County Club of Windsor. The ECC together with branch offices in Chatham, Sarnia, and Owen Sound served an area of approximately 680,000 people of which 44,683 were CAA members. The distribution of population and memberships among the four branches was as follows:

Branch	1970 Population[a]	Memberships
Essex (Windsor)	293,729	27,010
Kent (Chatham)	96,775	6,221
Lambton (Sarnia)	109,952	6,377
Blue Water (Owen Sound)	178,966	5,075

[a] SOURCE: Ontario Department of Municipal Affairs.

The primary approach used by the ECC to attract new members was telephone canvassing. Sales calls were made to people recommended by current members, and also to listings arbitrarily taken from the telephone directory. The telephone canvassing was supported by frequent billboard and newspaper advertisements.

Research Project

In early September, Mr. Savoie contacted a neighboring university and talked to one of the marketing professors. They agreed that a project for the ECC could make an interesting student research paper. A few days later Mr. Savoie was visited by a graduate business student, Mr. Andrew Spitz.

Mr. Savoie began the discussion by presenting the situation facing the ECC.

> *Mr. Savoie:* We feel our job is to provide good service, but we're not sure what services are most important to our members. We did a little survey this spring among some of our members. A list of eight major

services was prepared. These were mailed together with a membership brochure, and members were asked to rank the services in order of importance or appeal to them. We polled 2,990, or 10 percent, of our Master members and got a response of between 25 and 30 percent. Here is a summary showing the percent of respondents that ranked each service first, second, or third (Exhibit 6.1). As you can see, Emergency Road Service was rated highest.

Mr. Spitz: What other information does the ECC have on its members?

Mr. Savoie: Not much; for each member we have a record card that includes his or her address, type of membership, year joined, and renewal date.

As the discussion continued, Mr. Savoie introduced the problem of membership turnover.

Mr. Savoie: A major problem concerning us is turnover. For example, in the Essex office we lost approximately 2,300 members last year. This is compared to the 4,700 new members that we recruit.

Mr. Spitz: What do you think is the cause of nonrenewals?

Mr. Savoie: Our salesmen ask this when they are trying to get the renewal. The answers usually relate to money. Some say they can't afford membership any longer, or that they are not getting their money's worth. People seem to expect to save money by being members. In other words savings on services received must at least offset yearly membership costs. What they don't seem to understand is that they are buying insurance. They wouldn't expect to get tangible benefits equal to their annual life insurance premiums, would they?

Mr. Spitz No, I guess not. One thing is not clear to me. What happens to any profit or loss accruing to the ECC?

Mr. Savoie: We're completely nonprofit. We try to balance membership receipts and service expenses as closely as possible. Of course, we have a small buffer that carries over from year to year.

The rest of the discussion centered on how survey research could be used to help the ECC. Several interrelated areas seemed to be of primary interest. What driver segment had the ECC been able to attract? What were the reasons for nonrenewal of membership? How did drivers view the various club services? Finally, how could club membership be promoted?

Mr. Savoie indicated that a budget of 1,200 dollars had been made available for the research costs. He also indicated that time was not a major concern. It was agreed that Mr. Spitz would prepare a research proposal that would include a description of the proposed survey and an estimate of the research cost.

EXHIBIT 6.1
Summary Results
ECC Mail Survey of Members
(July 1971)

SERVICE	PERCENT RESPONDENTS WHO RANKED SERVICE 1st, 2nd, or 3rd [a]
1. Emergency road service	93.0
2. Legal assistance	52.3
3. Personal accident insurance	46.3
4. Trip planning	44.8
5. Bail and arrest bond	23.3
6. Substitute transportation	18.5
7. Trip guarantee service	17.2
8. Emergency cheque cashing	6.7

[a] Based on 749 replies from sample of 2990.

CASE 7

LIBB PHARMACEUTICALS ALIVE TOOTHPASTE

In terms of understanding consumer behavior and the subsequent formulation of marketing strategy, the measurement of consumer attitudes has become increasingly important. Many firms have found that it is valuable and necessary to know how consumers perceive their brands along key product attributes. At the same time it is of importance to know how competitors' brands are evaluated along the same attributes.

Management of Libb Pharmaceuticals became quite concerned when the market share of Alive toothpaste declined from about 15 percent to the present 10 percent. At a meeting of the product management team it was concluded that the firm should undertake some attitude research on the toothpaste market. Specifically the firm was interested in determining:

☐ What perceptions do people have of Alive toothpaste?
☐ What are the preferences for and perceptions of the other major brands of toothpaste?
☐ How can Alive toothpaste best be positioned in the marketplace?

Background Information

THE COMPANY

Libb Pharmaceuticals traces its origin back to 1855 when the founder, Phillip L. Libb, developed an all-purpose skin ointment. The product achieved relatively large success within a regional trading area. From the outset, Libb devoted a significant proportion of the firm's profits to the development of new product lines and the improvement of existing ones.

By the early 1900's the firm was manufacturing and distributing a wide line of pharmaceutical and personal care products. In addition, the firm was gradually expanding its marketing area and by 1920 had achieved national distribution for most of its products.

One of Libb's early product additions was in the area of toothpastes. At one point the firm was marketing four separate brands of toothpaste. By the end of World War II all of the brands had been gradually phased out with the exception of Alive. The decision was made at that time that Alive would be the firm's only brand of toothpaste and that it would be modified and reformulated as appropriate to keep the brand competitive with changing market conditions and potentials.

THE PRODUCT AND PROMOTION

At the present time, Alive toothpaste is being positioned almost as an all-in-one mouth care product. Promotional claims for the product include such statements as "Alive toothpaste polishes your teeth as bright as any other brands," "Alive contains special ingredients that freshen your breath like the leading mouthwashes," "Alive now contains a special fluoride to help reduce the threat of tooth decay," "Alive brightens and protects your teeth while it freshens your mouth."

Most of the brand's advertising budget is allocated to spot television commercials in both daytime and prime time. The basic themes of most commercials focus on boy meets girl and vice versa, and "slice of life" types of situations. The second largest share of the brands' advertising budget goes to national magazines with some use being made of Sunday newspaper supplements.

As another form of promotion, couponing, is utilized to some extent. Libb has also tried several promotional efforts where Alive toothpaste is associated with some of the firm's other products.

In essence the firm has made limited attempts to concentrate on any specific market segments with its promotional efforts. Instead, the focus has been on reaching as many consumers as possible with the amount of promotional dollars available.

Results of the Consumer Research

BRAND PREFERENCES

As another form of promotion, couponing is utilized to some extent. by 46.4 percent of the respondents. Alive was ranked first by 10.5 percent of the respondents, while 22.7 percent and 22.3 percent ranked it their second or third choice, respectively.

To gain a better understanding of brand preference across various levels of education a cross tabulation was developed as shown in Exhibit 7.2. It is significant to note that, in general, as education increases the preference for Alive decreases. This same phenomenon holds true for Colgate while the opposite is true for Crest.

ATTRIBUTE IMPORTANCES

As part of the input to the attitude model respondents were asked to rank the importance of five attributes of toothpaste. Exhibit 7.3 reports the ranking results for the total sample. Some 75 percent of the respondents ranked "Decay Prevention" as the most important attribute to them in selecting a brand of toothpaste. "Price" was ranked as least important.

CONSUMER PERCEPTIONS

The research team felt that the individual attribute ratings (question 1) would probably fairly represent the images and perceptions that consumers held toward the alternative brands studied. It was decided that the average consumer ratings for each attribute should be calculated for each brand. It was also concluded that these average ratings on each brand should be first computed for those who ranked the brand as their most preferred, and then computed for those who stated first preference for any of the other brands. The results of these calculations are shown in Exhibit 7.4.

Alive was rated as a 1.27 (the lower the rating the more satisfactory the brand is perceived on that attribute) on "Taste/Flavor" by those who prefer it and as a 2.23 by those who stated preference for some other brand. Respondents preferring Alive rated it as a 1.56 on "Decay Prevention" while those preferring Crest rated it as a 1.21 on that attribute.

EXHIBIT 7.1
Frequency of Brand Preference Rankings

	RANKING (IN PERCENT)				
BRANDS	*1st*	*2nd*	*3rd*	*4th*	*5th*
Gleem	9.0	28.1	25.0	29.9	8.0
Crest	46.4	19.6	19.8	9.8	4.4
Alive	10.5	22.7	22.3	30.1	14.5
Colgate	24.9	21.5	24.7	21.0	7.9
Macleans	9.2	8.2	8.2	9.2	65.2

EXHIBIT 7.2
Brand Preference Given Educational Level

	BRANDS PREFERRED (IN PERCENT)						
EDUCATIONAL LEVEL	Gleem	Crest	Alive	Colgate	Macleans	Others	
Some grammar school	5.5	18.4	16.6	44.8	2.7	12.0	100.0%
Completed grammar school	7.6	24.7	11.8	37.7	3.9	14.2	100.0%
Some high school	5.1	29.7	14.1	33.9	5.5	11.6	100.0%
Completed high school	5.1	33.4	10.9	31.5	5.9	13.2	100.0%
Some college	6.7	42.4	10.7	23.3	4.6	12.2	100.0%
Completed college	4.7	49.1	9.3	22.7	3.6	10.5	100.0%
Masters or doctorate degree	4.5	53.4	7.9	17.4	3.2	13.7	100.0%

EXHIBIT 7.3
Frequency of Attribute Importance Rankings

	RANKING (IN PERCENT)				
ATTRIBUTE	1st	2nd	3rd	4th	5th
Decay prevention	75.5	11.7	5.6	3.8	3.4
Taste/Flavor	11.4	26.1	24.8	25.9	11.8
Freshens mouth	4.3	21.8	32.8	32.0	9.1
Whitens teeth	5.9	31.1	23.6	22.9	16.5
Price	2.9	9.3	13.2	15.4	59.3

EXHIBIT 7.4
Average Consumer Ratings of Toothpaste Brands on Relevant Attributes

		AVERAGE SCORE ON				
BRANDS		Decay Prevention	Taste/ Flavor	Freshens Breath	Whitens Teeth	Price
Gleem	A [a]	1.83	1.33	1.33	1.78	1.95
	B [b]	2.64	2.26	2.06	2.34	2.27
Crest	A	1.21	1.32	1.44	1.99	1.96
	B	1.97	2.31	2.21	2.44	2.27
Alive	A	1.56	1.27	1.28	1.80	2.11
	B	2.40	2.23	2.13	2.45	2.24
Colgate	A	1.40	1.26	1.25	1.80	1.96
	B	2.39	2.04	1.98	2.50	2.24
Macleans	A	1.89	1.64	1.28	1.35	2.14
	B	3.03	3.39	2.66	2.38	2.50

[a] Row A = average ratings given the brand by respondents preferring *that brand.*
[b] Row B = average ratings given the brand by respondents preferring *any of the other brands.*

RESEARCH METHODOLOGY AND QUESTIONNAIRE

Four distinct steps were used in the development and execution of this toothpaste research. First, the relevant product attributes for toothpaste had to be determined. The second step involved designing the questions to be asked and testing consumers' ability and willingness to answer them. It was then necessary to test the overall questionnaire on a small sample under conditions similar to those that would prevail for the final survey. The last step was the nationwide administration of the final survey.

Product Attributes

The five product attributes used for toothpaste were ascertained from the results of 20 small, focus group interviews. These interviews took the form of getting consumers involved in a general discussion about those things that consumers think about when selecting a brand of toothpaste. The five attributes used in this study were the ones mentioned most frequently in these interviews: (1) decay prevention; (2) taste/flavor; (3) freshens mouth; (4) whitens teeth; and (5) price.

Initial Questionnaire

Once the relevant product attributes were decided upon, a sample questionnaire was constructed and tested on a group of consumers to determine their ability and willingness to answer the questions. The results of this informal test indicated that the respondents were in general able and willing to answer these types of questions.

The Pretest

In order to insure that individuals would respond to this type of questionnaire under actual field conditions, it was decided to run a pretest of 100 panel households. A cover letter accompanied the questionnaire providing information about how to fill it out along with an incentive to participate in the form of a promised gift upon return of the completed questionnaire. Approximately 68 percent of this sample returned the questionnaire within two weeks. In general the results were satisfactory with no more than the anticipated number of omissions. With minor rewording of some of the questions, it was decided to go ahead with the complete sample.

Final Questionnaire

The final questionnaire was mailed to 2,000 households who were members of a national mail panel. The households were selected to provide a balanced sample which paralleled census data for the United States with respect to geographic divisions, and within each division by total household income, population density, degree of urbanization, and age of panel member. In each case the questionnaire was to be completed by the female head-of-household. Each respondent was offered a small gift (retail value of about $2.00) for cooperating with the research. Within the predetermined six-week cut-off period, 78.5 percent of the 2,000 households had responded to the questionnaire. However, out of these 1,571 returned questionnaires, only 1,272 or 63.6 percent of the total sample were deemed usable for the entire analysis.

Basic Questions

In addition to the standard demographic characteristics, the following questions were asked of each respondent:

1. Now we would like for you to think about these attributes for the leading brands of toothpaste. Circle a "1" if you think the brand is very satisfactory in the attribute, "6" if you think it is very *un*satisfactory in the attribute, or somewhere in between depending how well you are satisfied with the brand. *Please indicate your "feelings" about the brand even though you have not tried it or do not currently use it.*

GLEEM	*Satisfactory*					*Unsatisfactory*
Decay prevention	1	2	3	4	5	6
Taste/Flavor	1	2	3	4	5	6
Freshens mouth	1	2	3	4	5	6
Whitens teeth	1	2	3	4	5	6
Price	1	2	3	4	5	6
CREST	*Satisfactory*					*Unsatisfactory*
Decay prevention	1	2	3	4	5	6
Taste/Flavor	1	2	3	4	5	6
Freshens mouth	1	2	3	4	5	6
Whitens teeth	1	2	3	4	5	6
Price	1	2	3	4	5	6
ALIVE	*Satisfactory*					*Unsatisfactory*
Decay prevention	1	2	3	4	5	6
Taste/Flavor	1	2	3	4	5	6
Freshens mouth	1	2	3	4	5	6
Whitens teeth	1	2	3	4	5	6
Price	1	2	3	4	5	6
COLGATE	*Satisfactory*					*Unsatisfactory*
Decay prevention	1	2	3	4	5	6
Taste/Flavor	1	2	3	4	5	6
Freshens mouth	1	2	3	4	5	6
Whitens teeth	1	2	3	4	5	6
Price	1	2	3	4	5	6

MACLEANS	Satisfactory					Unsatisfactory
Decay prevention	1	2	3	4	5	6
Taste/Flavor	1	2	3	4	5	6
Freshens mouth	1	2	3	4	5	6
Whitens teeth	1	2	3	4	5	6
Price	1	2	3	4	5	6

2. Please rank the following attributes for toothpaste in their order of importance to you in selecting a brand. Write a "1" by the attribute which is most important to you, a "2" by the attribute which is next most important to you, and so on until you have ranked all five attributes.

——————Decay prevention
——————Taste/Flavor
——————Freshens mouth
——————Whitens teeth
——————Price

3. Now, we would like for you to rank these five brands of toothpaste by writing a "1" next to your favorite brand, a "2" next to your second favorite brand, and so on. If your favorite brand is not listed, please write it in the space provided. However, still rank the given brands in order of preference from 1 to 5 even if you are not currently using them.

——————Gleem
——————Crest
——————Alive
——————Colgate
——————Macleans
——————————————Preferred Brand

4. How many times a day is toothpaste used by all members of your family counted together?

Don't use——————   1 to 2——————   7 to 8——————
                              3 to 4——————   9 to 10——————
                              5 to 6——————   More than 10——————

PART THREE
PRODUCT STRATEGY

CASE 8

GENERAL CONSUMER APPLIANCES
PRODUCT STRATEGY AND CHANGING VALUES

General Consumer Products has long been a leader in the area of developing and marketing small appliances consistent with the changing needs and value systems of consumers. In today's era of rapid and in some instances accelerating change, however, it is becoming increasingly difficult to monitor and respond to true shifts in the prevailing consumer attitudes.

The following sections briefly summarize the notes taken by Eric Roper, Director of new product development for General Consumer Products, at a one-day seminar focusing on changing values and lifestyles. As he reviews the notes he is interested in identifying new product opportunities which would enable his firm to better serve the emerging lifestyles of consumers.

Key Market Trends

We are living in a period of relative affluence. The average family in 1980 will be better off financially, even after inflation, than the average family in 1970. Much of the increase in average family income will be due to an increasing number of multiple-wage-earner families. This typically means that the wife is also employed outside the home.

A larger portion of the before-tax income will be concentrated among the younger market segments in 1980 as compared to 1970. This is due to the increasing number of people in the 20 to 34 age group. In 1980 there will be about 55 percent more people in the 25 to 34 age group than there were in 1968. In addition, these consumers tend to be better educated than their earlier counterparts and as a result command larger salaries earlier in their careers.

There is also the phenomena known as the "trickle-up" theory which suggests that values and attitudes tend to originate among the younger segments of our society and are passed up, at least in moderation, to the older segments. This theory has been suggested based on recent trends in clothing, hair styles, sexual mores, and a variety of prevailing attitudes in our society. In many ways we represent a society in the pursuit of youth. At the same time it is important to note that "youth" is not just an age category. More importantly it represents a state of mind, a set of attitudes.

Basic Motivating Forces Behind Change

Many of the changes today have come about because of changes in the "cultural transfusive triad," those three elements of society—family, church, and school—that transfuse values from one generation to another. In many ways the family and church represent less influence on the transmission of values and attitudes today than in the past while schools are considered by many to be more of an influence.

The family is considered to be *less* of an influence because there is limited contact between one generation and another since members of the younger generation tend to move away from their home towns after completing their educations; children are exposed to the education system at a much earlier age than was true in the past; the traditional roles of mother and father are changing; an increasing number of mothers are employed outside the home; many fathers are essentially only "weekend fathers" because of responsibilities associated with their careers; the divorce rate is rising; and a variety of other factors.

The church is considered to be *less* of an influence because of: a general decline in church membership and attendance in recent years, especially among the Catholics and younger segments of society; an even greater decline in Sunday school attendance; an increasing perception on the part of many people that religion is becoming less of an influence upon society; and growing disenchantment among those in the clergy. The "Jesus Revolution" may be a counter trend but to date has involved a relatively small percentage of the youth and has been, in general, outside the organized church.

The school is considered to be *more* of an influence because of; a new breed of teachers who present a broader range of backgrounds, values, and attitudes to the students than has been true in the past; and a movement toward an analytical approach to education which focuses more on evaluation and understanding rather than memorization and regurgitation.

Changing Lifetime Experiences

Many of the younger people today grew up with television as opposed to being introduced to it as were their parents. Television and other mass media have greatly speeded up the transmission of change in values and attitudes.

We also need to realize that almost half the people alive today were not alive when World War II ended. This post-war generation knows little of the impact of the Great Depression and World War II upon the society. Instead they have existed in a period of almost uninterrupted, relative affluence. Their lifetime experiences have, however, been significant. This generation has experienced and endured such critical events as the nuclear age, the civil rights movement, great concern over poverty, space exploration, the Vietnam War, concern about ecology, university experiences, the communications revolution, Watergate, etc.

They have emerged with a set of key perspectives which include: the belief that national priorities are inverted, a distaste for social rigidity, a concern about institutional rigidity, a feeling of lack of political influence and power, a loss of *self* to technology and institutions, an intolerance of hypocrisy, and an absence of meaningful relationships. Again, because of the trickle-up effect, the attitudes and values of this younger generation have been passed on, at least in moderation, to the preceding generation.

Emerging Lifestyles

Key market trends, changes in the family, church, and school, and varying lifetime experiences combine to create a variety of emerging lifestyles. These lifestyles are partially listed and briefly described below.

Instant Gratification.   People used to be willing to wait a long time to satisfy their personal and consumption problems; today they want to be satisfied right away.

Credit Explosion.   In the past, debt was something that should be avoided, or at least minimized; today consumers are much more willing to purchase on credit.

New Theology of Pleasure.   There has been a decline in the Puritan ethic and a movement toward "if it feels good, do it."

New Work Ethic.   Margaret Mead summarizes this by stating, "People used to live to work. Now they work in order to live."

Life Simplification.   Consumers are interested in products and services that take the work out of life, that allow them to do things quicker and easier, that save them physical energy and time.

Morality Revolution.   Fundamental changes are occurring in the moral attitudes of consumers; sexual approaches to advertising, provided they are in "good taste," are being increasingly accepted as communication themes.

Changing Feminity.   The role of women in society is changing; more are working outside the home and are involved in a variety of occupations and activities which were formerly closed or limited to them.

Family Trends.   Younger families tend to spend less time with members of their preceding generation, but are becoming more oriented toward sharing time with their own children.

Youth Orientation.   In the past it was often desirable to appear older and distinguished; today the orientation is more toward looking and acting youthful.

Appearance and Health.   Consumers are becoming increasingly concerned about their physical appearance and health.

Introspection.   As a result of the declining influence of the church and the changes in moral attitudes, people are searching for new standards and codes.

Novelty, Change, and Escape.   Many consumers are interested in products which provide a novelty or change of pace or even an escape from their regular life existence.

Naturalism.   Many consumers are rejecting artificial forms of behavior and appearances in favor of naturalism.

Personal Creativity.   Large segments of consumers are looking for products which enable them to exhibit their personal creativity.

Fear.   People do not like to talk about this but it is becoming increasingly important. Many people are afraid to walk alone at nights in their own neighborhood; the crime rate is up dramatically in all areas of criminal offenses.

Institutional Reliance.   It used to be that individuals were supposed to take care of themselves, but increasingly people now rely on institutions to solve their problems.

Loss of Confidence in Institutions.   It is somewhat ironic that while people are relying more heavily on institutions to solve their problems, they also have become less confident of the ability of institutions to satisfy them.

Energy Conservation.   Consumers are seeking products and services which enable them to save on energy consumption.

Consumerism.   People are becoming more concerned about their rights as consumers; the rights of safety, of being heard, of choosing, and of obtaining information as originally stated by President John F. Kennedy in 1962.

CASE 9

LIFE RESTAURANT NUTRITIONAL AND HEALTHFUL DINING

Over a period of several years, Dan Williams, an optometry student, and his wife, Christina, a dental hygienist, developed an interest in owning and operating their own restaurant. Dan obtained some experience in the field having worked as a waiter and bartender in several restaurants and Christina had read a great deal of literature on health foods and good nutritional habits. It was a merging of their interests and experiences that led them to formulate plans for Life Restaurant.

The basic image of the restaurant would be one of good nutrition and well-balanced meals accompanied by natural surroundings. Strategy called for having food nutritionists on the staff to assure that consumers would be offered meals with proper amounts of vitamins, protein, fats, carbohydrates, and calories. Exterior and interior design would be planned to present a pleasant, natural atmosphere emphasizing the beauty of life itself.

Dan and Christina saw the restaurant as not only selling food and accompanying services, but also as promoting good health, and in a subtle way, as educating the public on proper nutrition. The proposed menu was planned to include foods consistent with the "American style" of dining, such as steaks, seafood, and poultry items. Each, however, would be prepared in such a way as to provide for maximum nutritional value. An extensive salad bar would be available for each customer to prepare his or her own salad. Proposed desserts would include such items as yogurt parfaits (high in protein) and homemade peanut butter ice cream pie (high in protein, magnesium, vitamin A, and calories).

Philosophy of Life Restaurant[1]

[1]The following material has been extracted from a descriptive brochure designed to raise financial support for the restaurant.

Throughout their history, restaurants have flourished at the customer's expense—*not* an expense in terms of money, but a greater one in the abuse of their health. Traditionally, restaurants have always encouraged the sale of unnecessary cocktails that hog the calorie count better reserved for nutritious foods; they pamper the customer with tempting entree offerings that are too often fried and greasy, and then assault the body with fattening, cholesterol-clogged desserts.

Restaurants, in short, don't really care about people; they care about customers. They are food "merchandisers," concerned with *selling* food—the more, the better. They pamper the most childish part of the customer, giving him sweets and fats and goodies—all those noxious and unwholesome things we have been taught to think of as desirable—but giving little consideration to his intelligence, and showing utter indifference to his health.

Today, the communication media are educating people in the importance of diet. Our concern for environment pollution is matched by an ever-growing concern for the inner pollution of our bodies. Although television, radio, newspapers, and magazines everywhere give voice to this concern, it seems that one group of people—restaurant owners—have not heard and will not listen. It is time that such a loud and clear message *is* heard, and it is important that the rapidly expanding dining public find out that there is a restaurant for people, not customers. The answer to this deep and pervasive need is *Life.*

The message of *Life* is that of wholesomeness, of vitality, of a clean and elegant atmosphere in which delicious and well-balanced meals are served. With no sacrifice of taste and those culinary graces that distinguish good dining from mere eating, *Life* accepts the responsibility that its name suggests: *Life's* meals are nutritional and healthful. In contrast to the stomach-souring, artery-clogging pollutants served by most restaurants, the food served at *Life* is a vitality food, it is digestable and nourishing . . . it is life.

Each customer begins his meal with a multiple vitamin tablet to give immediate and tangible insurance that his body will be well fortified with these "life helpers," vitamins. The short-term menu includes high-quality protein foods—lean steaks, prime ribs, poultry, and fish—all prepared to keep nutrients in and fat and cholesterol out. Moderate carbohydrates are available in a whole baked potato and enriched breads. A plenitude of extra vitamins and minerals is available at the salad bar, where the customer is invited to make his own salad from the wholesome variety of fresh vegetables, cool fruits, relishes, and dressings.

Whereas most restaurants hardsell their cocktails for profit, *Life* makes cocktails available for those who so desire, but does not promote them merely to fatten the check. Instead, in its emphasis, *Life* has returned to the older traditions of festive dining and includes a cold pitcher of beer or a carafe of natural wine with each meal. Children's portions are available at half-price, and include a kiddie cocktail of fruit juices; thus they emphasize in simply one more way *Life's* concern for *people,* which means children and the whole family, just as it includes the individual customer's total welfare, not simply his palate and pocketbook.

An added beauty of *Life* is its architectural design and the light, open, and free atmosphere within. Courtyards with a natural setting of live green plants and flowers to cool and refresh the eye are visible from every table. Live fountains with flowing water in these courtyards enhance the peaceful beauty that is so conducive to the charm and satisfaction of good dining.

The four dining areas, each with a capacity of 25, are bordered by both inner and outer courtyards, giving to every seating location a spirit of openness and freedom. Natural lighting is provided by the soft candlelight inside blending with the filtered daylight from without.

In the establishment of each new *Life* restaurant, a new and wholesome choice is made available to thousands of people for that invigorating celebration of healthful and gracious living that good dining is meant to be.

CASE 10

DOW CHEMICAL COMPANY[1]

DOW DOMES

Dow Domes are an effective, economical, and aesthetically satisfying solution to a variety of problems requiring a strong but lightweight dome-shaped structure. These structures have enjoyed an excellent growth rate for Dow over the past years, and management sees the future as quite attractive for its existing markets of water and sewage treatment plants.

The firm is concerned, however, that it may be necessary to modify its approach to this market in terms of selling effort and advertising approaches in order to meet the challenge of alternative domes on the market. Many of these domes are less expensive but not of equal quality to a Dow Dome. However, some manufacturers of these domes are constantly pushing to have the specifiers (architects, consulting engineers, etc.) consider their product as equal. Management of Dow is also interested in expanding its base of operations into other markets for domes.

[1]This case originally appeared in *Contemporary Cases in Marketing* by W. Wayne Talarzyk (Hinsdale, Ill.: The Dryden Press, 1974).

Product Information

PRODUCT DEVELOPMENT

The history of Dow Domes started in 1959 when Donald R. Wright, a Dow engineer, was building a snow igloo for his children. He used an inverted trough, which he moved in circles to distribute the snow needed to construct the igloo. When it was finished he had the forerunner of the Dow Dome. Extensive development tests carried on by Wright and other Dow engineers showed that by using an 8-inch thickness of Styrofoam,[2] bonded by heat, domes up to 90 feet in diameter could be constructed. Later developments, including the addition of reinforced steel wire, allowed for the construction of domes up to 200 feet in diameter. The first commercialization of this product was in 1964. Since that time over 100 Dow Domes have been constructed. Exhibit 10.1 shows a photograph of 27 Dow Domes, ranging in size from 50 to 168 feet in diameter, covering circular structures as the Cedar Rapids, Iowa Water Pollution Control Plant.

PRODUCT CHARACTERISTICS

The Dow Dome is a thin shell of reinforced, high-strength, latex-modified cement covering a Styrofoam brand plastic foam base. These domes are strong enough to withstand high winds and heavy snow loads, but light enough to be placed upon most existing foundations. When conditions dictate, Dow Domes can be constructed in place, with process interruptions at treatment plants measured in days rather than the weeks required for alternative structures. In many cases, Dow Domes can be constructed near the treatment facility and lifted into place and installed on a circular structure with virtually no process interruption.

The insulation properties of Styrofoam brand plastic foam are extremely effective, therefore eliminating the hazardous manual deicing techniques usually employed at treatment plants. In addition, Dow Domes are practically maintenance free. There are no moving parts to maintain or replace and no interior finish is necessary. Since the domes are not affected by moisture, rot, or corrosion, frequent repainting is not required. Exhibit 10.2 shows some of the structural properties of the domes.

TECHNIQUE OF CONSTRUCTION

The Dow Domes are constructed at the customer's location by Dow's own construction people. Construction begins with the assembly of a steel starter ring on a site adjacent to the installation site. (In some instances, the domes are constructed in place.) A temporary pad of concrete is poured in the center of the ring to support the spinning equipment. The basic form is

[2]Trademark of Dow Chemical Company.

constructed of Styrofoam brand extruded polystyrene foam, utilizing a unique construction process developed by Dow Chemical known as "Spiral Generation." As the spinning booms move along, as shown in Exhibit 10.3, boards of Styrofoam are fed by the operator into the welding machine.

The contacting surfaces are heated to the fusion point and pressed together by the weight of the welding machine to form a thermal weld. Steel wires are implanted at regular intervals to further strengthen the dome. With the crane moving at approximately 30 feet per minute, a five-man crew can cover up to 7,000 square feet in a 14-hour day.

After each dome is spun, it is lifted by crane onto the existing foundation. Next, openings are cut for doors, windows, and vents and the frames set in place. The starter ring is then welded to the anchoring plates, as shown in Exhibit 10.4. As the next step, self-furring, steel reinforcing mesh is fastened to the dome. Later, layers of a high-bonding, latex-modified cement are applied to the exterior of each dome to form the structural shell.

Marketing Environment
MARKET SEGMENTS

The primary use for Dow Domes today is covering circular process units at water and sewage treatment plants. In water plants, the need is for protective cover for a potable water supply. In sewage treatment plants, the primary need is for the control of odor emanating from various process units. By utilizing a Dow Dome, the odors are contained. Other equipment can then be used to treat the odors and vent the air into the atmosphere. In certain climates, it is also necessary to cover sewage treatment facilities to control fogging and icing conditions.

Dow Domes also find application in the architectural area for use as auditoriums, bulk storage facilities, and other similar structures. In the architectural field, the insulating value of the form of Styrofoam is of value to the customer.

THE COMPETITION

There are several other manufacturers and constructors of dome structures. These range from products that are less expensive than a Dow Dome to other products that are more expensive. Some examples of these products are as follows: air-inflated balloon-type structures, glass fiber domes, reinforced concrete domes utilizing conventional construction techniques, steel and aluminum domes using truss sections and panels, wood domes of similar construction, and geodesic domes utilizing a space frame of either aluminum or steel and panels of various construction materials such as glass fiber, plexiglass, aluminum, and steel.

DOW'S MARKETING STRATEGY

Dow Domes as of 1975 are being marketed by the sales force of the Environmental Control Systems Division of Dow Chemical. These salesmen are involved in several aspects of the pollution control field and are in contact with the key buying influences (municipalities, consulting engineers, and architects) on a daily basis.

Dow is aggressively pursuing the odor control market where the needs are relatively well defined. The architectural market is vast, but consists of many small jobs and is not as economically attractive. The larger architectural applications, on the other hand, represent an attractive potential.

The company is currently using advertising, promotional case histories placed in key magazines, and direct-mail programs to assist in the marketing of this product. The first two are used to give Dow Domes a general exposure in the marketplace. The direct-mail program is targeted specifically to individuals who can influence the sale of this product.

EXHIBIT 10.1
Photograph of Installation of Dow Domes
(Cedar Rapids, Iowa Water Pollution Control Plant)

EXHIBIT 10.2
Structural Properties of Dow Domes

TYPICAL SHELL THICKNESS SELECTION TABLE
STANDARD 50° DOME

Dome Plan Diameter (ft.)	Foam Shell Thickness (in.)	LMC Shell Thickness (in.)
0-30	4	¾
31-40	4	¾
41-50	4	¾
51-60	4	¾
61-80	6	¾
81-130	8	¾
131-140	8	⅞
141-160	8	1
161-180	8	1⅛
181-190	8	1¼
191-200	8	1⅜

DESIGN CRITERIA

Foam Shell	LMC Shell
Dead Load—2 pcf	Dead Load—145 pcf (Seldom exceeds 15 psf)
Construction Live Load—15 psf (min.)	Live Load
	Snow—30 psf
	Wind—20 psf (100 mph wind)

MATERIAL PHYSICAL PROPERTIES

Material	Compressive Strength	Tensile Strength	Elastic Modulus
Foam*	30 psi	60 psi	2,000 psi
LMC	4,130 psi	790 psi	1,920,000 psi

* STYROFOAM® brand extruded polystyrene foam.

EXHIBIT 10.3
"Spiral Generation" Construction of the Dome

EXHIBIT 10.4
Mounting Detail of the Dome

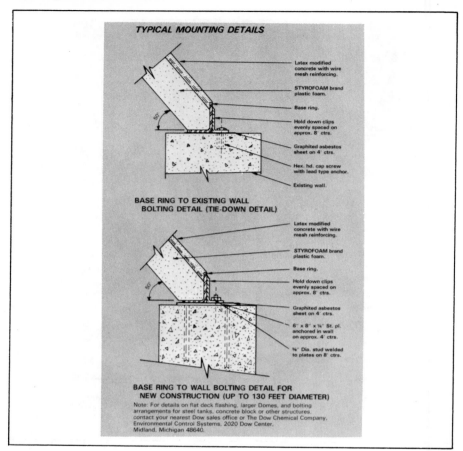

TYPICAL MOUNTING DETAILS

Latex modified concrete with wire mesh reinforcing.

STYROFOAM brand plastic foam.

Base ring.

Hold down clips evenly spaced on approx. 8' ctrs.

Graphited asbestos sheet on 4' ctrs.

Hex. hd. cap screw with lead type anchor.

Existing wall.

**BASE RING TO EXISTING WALL
BOLTING DETAIL (TIE-DOWN DETAIL)**

Latex modified concrete with wire mesh reinforcing.

STYROFOAM brand plastic foam.

Base ring.

Hold down clips evenly spaced on approx. 8' ctrs.

Graphited asbestos sheet on 4' ctrs.

6" × 8" × ¼" St. pl. anchored in wall on approx. 4' ctrs.

¾" Dia. stud welded to plates on 8' ctrs.

**BASE RING TO WALL BOLTING DETAIL FOR
NEW CONSTRUCTION (UP TO 130 FEET DIAMETER)**

Note: For details on flat deck flashing, larger Domes, and bolting arrangements for steel tanks, concrete block or other structures, contact your nearest Dow sales office or The Dow Chemical Company, Environmental Control Systems, 2020 Dow Center, Midland, Michigan 48640.

PART FOUR
DISTRIBUTION STRATEGY

PART FOUR

CASE 11

JS&A NATIONAL SALES GROUP

SPACE-AGE ELECTRONIC CONSUMER PRODUCTS

The JS&A National Sales Group was America's largest single source of electronic calculators and is now a leading specialist in the evaluation and marketing of the nation's new micro-electronic space-age consumer products. Among the firm's early credits include the national introduction of the country's first electronic pocket calculator. It also pioneered the introduction of the new watch technology in the United States.

As one of the nation's largest exclusive direct marketing organizations, the firm's advertising has appeared in every major national business publication. In the *Wall Street Journal,* JS&A commands the number one position as the publication's largest mail-order advertiser and one of the top fourteen national advertisers along with IBM, IT&T, and other major firms.

Formation of the Company

Joseph Sugarman, an electrical engineering graduate who formerly worked as a CIA agent in Germany, returned to Oak Park, Illinois in 1965 and started his own advertising agency. In 1971, one of his clients, a direct-mail business, decided not to follow Sugarman's advice on the marketing of pocket electronic calculators. Even the manufacturer did not seem to sense the product's vast sales potential.

Sugarman then convinced the manufacturer, Craig Corporation, to let him introduce the calculator and then proceeded to raise money for his own direct-mail campaign. Within ten days and $12,000, a full-color flyer extolling the virtues of the country's first pocket calculator was mailed to 50,000 people. The initial price of the calculator was $239.95. After the price dropped to $179.95, Sugarman sent a second mailing to one million general business executives.

These two mailings yielded a profit for the fledgling company and Sugarman began searching for calculators and other products using the micro-electronic integrated circuit—the "brain" of the calculator. Today, the firm is the country's largest single source of electronic space-age products such as calculators, digital watches, and personal communication equipment. Gross sales of $100 million are projected for 1976.

Marketing Philosophy[1]

In an article in *Marketing News* Sugarman briefly outlined his "formula" for successful direct marketing. It included:

- ☐ Handle only a few space-age, micro-electronic products at a time.
- ☐ Test the products before marketing them.
- ☐ Write ads informative enough and candid enough to please consumerists.
- ☐ Test the ads.
- ☐ Be honest with customers.
- ☐ Sell for cash (or credit cards) only, never on an open-account basis, no matter how rich or prestigious the customer and that includes the federal government.
- ☐ Be a good customer of the telephone company.
- ☐ Keep your inventory only about a day, which is possible only because you know exactly what response your ads will bring in.

The firm attempts to show its customers great respect in every phase of a transaction from the speed with which their orders are processed to their treatment after a purchase. Orders are generally processed and shipped within 48 hours from JS&A's warehouse and all service requests are handled the day they are received. All JS&A customers have the option of returning their purchase for a prompt refund if they are not absolutely

---

[1]Portions of this section are paraphrased from "Space-age product marketer uses 1,000 word ads and toll-free numbers," by Bernice Finkelman, *Marketing News,* November 7, 1975, p. 7.

satisfied. Defective merchandise is picked up at the customer's door at the firm's expense and promptly replaced. The company's national 800 number watts line enables customers direct access to its entire organization. Customers can check on an order or receive additional information, all at the firm's expense. Any complaint is brought immediately to Sugarman or a top corporate officer who personally responds with prompt action.

JS&A does not accept open accounts (anything that involves purchase orders and billings instead of immediate payment) because it found such accounts were making 80 percent of the problems and only bringing in 20 percent of the profits. The firm does accept credit cards since those companies do the collecting from their customers.

Advertising Strategy

Sugarman says, "I feel that testing is one of the most important aspects of the mail-order business. I always test, no matter how hot I feel the product is." The firm's usual test vehicle is the Southwest edition of the *Wall Street Journal.* The response to this advertisement usually tells Sugarman how the product will do nationally.

A wholly owned subsidiary, JS&A Advertising, is an accredited, full-service advertising agency responsible for the firm's total advertising program. Much of the copy writing, art work, photography, layout, and even typesetting is still done by Sugarman himself.

Typical JS&A advertisements, containing about 1,000 words, are designed to tell the reader everything he or she needs to know about a relatively complicated product. The advertisements are easy to understand and ring with the writer's sincerity—a man vitally involved in introducing the consumer to the excitement of the growing space-age product revolution. A typical advertisement for a calculator is shown in Exhibit 11.1.

The firm advertises primarily in national newspapers such as the *Wall Street Journal, The New York Times,* and the *National Observer* as well as a wide range of consumer magazines including, *Time, Forbes, Business Week, Travel & Leisure, Scientific American, Playboy, Psychology Today, Rotarian, National Geographic, Money, Fortune,* and many others.

Pocket-size Citizens Band Transceivers

One of JS&A's newest products is "PocketCom," the world's first complete solid-state two-channel Citizens Band (CB) transceiver that fits into a pocket. It can be used as a paging system, intercom, or a pocket-size communications link for business or pleasure. An advertisement for this product is shown in Exhibit 11.2.

According to Sugarman,

The PocketCom with its new integrated electronic circuitry represents the most important major breakthrough in personal communications since the advent of the transistor. We feel it ranks equal in importance with the development of the micro-electronic calculator itself. PocketCom ushers in an era of truly portable personal communication.

EXHIBIT 11.1
A Typical Advertisement for a JS&A Product

Presenting America's First
Human CALCULATOR

Three major design breakthroughs and a one year insurance policy humanizes the answer to the four most common calculator errors.

You're human! You make mistakes. And finally a company has come up with a calculator that realizes this.

ERROR 1: Oops, I forgot to shut it off!
Ever forget to turn off your calculator? Chances are, even if you're careful, you've made that mistake. The Litronix 2230 actually turns itself off. After one minute of unattended use, a small integrated timing circuit causes the display to blink on for one second and shut off for three seconds, thus conserving power without affecting the data. Then after 15 minutes, it shuts off completely.

LITRONIX L.E.D. DISPLAY

`1 2 3 · 4 5 6 7 8`

CONVENTIONAL L.E.D. DISPLAY

`1 2 3 . 4 5 6 7 8`

The Litronix "digit-position" floating decimal provides a clear distinction between the whole number and the decimal on the display.

ERROR 2: Oops, I read the decimal wrong!
Litronix has developed an eight-digit display whose decimal is in the center of a digit position, automatically separating the whole numbers from the decimals by the widest margin of any display. So there's no guesswork when it comes to spotting your decimal.

ERROR 3: Oops, I dropped it!
You're stepping out of your car, your briefcase flies open and out falls your calculator onto the solid cement walk. No problem with the Litronix. Just pick up the pieces, mail it to Litronix and they'll send you a brand new one anytime during the one year warranty period. It's the first pocket calculator actually insured against accidents.

BUT THERE'S SO MUCH MORE
We've told you how we've humanized the electronic calculator but there are many other exciting features:

Easy-to-use The Litronix features algebraic logic which means that you perform the functions exactly as you think.

Three key memory The memory system has three separate keys for data entry. You can

The keyboard on the Litronix was patterned after the expensive Hewlett Packard unit and has a three button color-coded memory system. Instead of the conventional on/off switch the Litronix has on/off keys.

now do calculations on your display, store the answers in a memory bank, and recall their total without erasing what was previously stored.

More hidden features The separate "on-key" replaces the standard "on-switch" thus eliminating a calculator's only moving part (a major cause of calculator problems).

The Litronix has a true automatic constant on all five functions and can do reciprocals, raise numbers to whole powers, compute square roots, and show overflow conditions. In addition, there's a floating negative sign, sign change feature, exchange key and a percentage system that gives intermediate percentage results with each calculation. You can do invoice extensions, compound interest problems, or many other business and scientific calculations.

AVAILABLE IN RECHARGEABLE OR DISPOSABLE BATTERY OPTIONS
The Litronix 2230's each price is only $29.95 complete with carrying case and three disposable AA cell batteries. The battery-saving features and the low-drain circuit will give many hours of carefree use. An AC adapter is free with the unit.

The new Litronix memory calculator has no moving parts, shuts itself off, and floats a decimal like no other pocket calculator. It weighs 6 ounces and measures only 3/4" x 3 1/8" x 6 1/2".

TWO WEEK FREE TRIAL $29⁹⁵

The Litronix 2230R (the exact same unit) is only $39.95 and comes complete with carrying case, rechargeable batteries, and AC adapter/charger. If you use your calculator daily in its portable mode, the rechargeable version is the better option. Both units are backed by a solid one year Litronix warranty and a prompt Litronix service-by-mail facility.

Credit card buyers may call our toll-free number below or send us your check or money order including $2.50 for postage and handling (Illinois residents add 5% sales tax). Please specify the option you wish, and we'll rush your unit out by return mail.

IT'S ONLY HUMAN
Finally, one of the very best calculators you can buy is also easy to operate and totally worry-free. What a refreshing change! Why not pick up your phone and order one at no obligation today.

JS&A NATIONAL SALES GROUP
Dept. SPG   JS&A Plaza
Northbrook, Illinois 60062
CALL TOLL-FREE . . 800 323-6400
In Illinois call . . . . (312) 498-6900
©JS&A Group, Inc., 1976

EXHIBIT 11.2
Introductory Advertisement for the PocketCom

Pocket CB

Talk to the world with a new citizens band transceiver that fits in your pocket.

The Dick Tracy wrist radio may no longer be a dream. Mega Corporation proudly introduces the PocketCom—a new tiny personal communications system that actually fits in your pocket.

MANY PERSONAL USES

An executive can now talk anywhere with anybody in his office, his factory or job site. The housewife can find her children at a busy shopping center. The motorist can signal for help in an emergency. The salesman, the construction foreman, the traveler, the sportsman, the hobbyist—everybody can use the PocketCom—as a pager, an intercom, a telephone or even a security device.

LONG RANGE COMMUNICATIONS

The PocketCom's range is limited only by its 100 milliwatt power and the number of metal objects between units or from a few blocks in the city to five miles on a lake. Its receiver is so sensitive, that signals several miles away can be picked up from stronger citizens band base stations.

VERY SIMPLE OPERATION

To use the PocketCom simply turn it on, extend the antenna, press a button to transmit, and release it to listen. And no FCC license is required to operate it. The PocketCom has two Channels—channel 14 and an optional second channel. To use the second channel, plug in one of the 22 other citizens band crystals and slide the channel selector to the second position. Crystals for the second channel cost $7.95 and can only be ordered after receipt of your unit.

BEEP-TONE PAGING SYSTEM

You can page another PocketCom user, within close range, by simply pressing the PocketCom's call button which produces a beep tone on the other unit if it has been left in the standby mode. In the standby mode the unit is silent and can be kept on for weeks without draining the batteries.

A MAJOR BREAKTHROUGH

The PocketCom's small size results from a breakthrough in the solid state device that made the pocket calculator a reality. Mega scientists took 112 transistors, integrated them on a micro silicon wafer and produced the world's first transceiver linear integrated circuit. This major breakthrough not only reduced the size of radio components but improved their dependability and performance. A large and expensive walkie talkie costing several hundred dollars might have only 12 transistors compared to 112 in the Mega PocketCom.

SUPERIOR FEATURES

Just check the advanced PocketCom features now possible through this new circuit breakthrough: 1) Incoming signals are amplified several million times compared to only 100,000 times on comparable conventional systems. 2) Even with a 60 decibel difference in signal strength, the unit's automatic gain control will bring up each incoming signal to a maximum uniform level. 3) A high squelch sensitivity (0.7 microvolts) permits noiseless operation without squelching weak signals. 4)

Harmonic distortion is so low that it far exceeds EIA (Electronic Industries Association) standards whereas most comparable systems don't even meet EIA specification. 5) The receiver has better than one microvolt sensitivity.

EXTRA LONG BATTERY LIFE

The PocketCom has a light-emitting diode low-battery indicator that tells you when your 'N' cell batteries require replacement. The integrated circuit requires such low power that the two batteries, with average use, will last weeks without running down.

| EXECUTIVES | POLICE | MOTORISTS |
| SHOPPERS | HIKERS | FOREMEN |

The PocketCom is used as a pager, an intercom, a telephone or even a security device.

MULTIPLEX INTERCOM

Many businesses can use the PocketCom as a multiplex intercom. Each employee carries a unit tuned to a different channel. A stronger citizens band base station with 23 channels is used to page each PocketCom. The results: an inexpensive and flexible multiplex intercom system for large construction sites, factories, offices, or farms.

NATIONAL SERVICE

The PocketCom is manufactured exclusively for JS&A by Mega Corporation. JS&A is America's largest supplier of space-age products and Mega Corporation is a leading manufacturer of innovative personal communication systems—further assurance that your modest investment is well protected. The PocketCom should give you years of trouble-free service, however, should service ever be required, simply slip your 5 ounce Pocket-Com into its handy mailer and send it to Mega's prompt national service-by-mail center. It is just that easy.

GIVE IT A REAL WORKOUT

Remember the first time you saw a pocket calculator? It probably seemed unbelievable. The PocketCom may also seem unbelieveable so we give you the opportunity to personally examine one without obligation. Order only two units on a trial basis. Then really test them. Test the range, the sensitivity, the convenience. Test them under your working conditions and compare the PocketCom with larger units that sell for several hundred dollars.

After you are absolutely convinced that the PocketCom is indeed that advanced product breakthrough, order your additional units, crystals or accessories on a priority basis as one of our established customers. If, however, the PocketCom does not suit your particular

The PocketCom measures approximately ¾" x 1½" x 5½" and easily fits into your shirt pocket. The unit can be used as a personal communications link for business or pleasure.

requirements perfectly, then return your units within ten days after receipt for a prompt and courteous refund. You cannot lose. Here is your opportunity to test an advanced space-age product at absolutely no risk.

A COMPLETE PACKAGE

Each PocketCom comes complete with mercury batteries, high performance Channel 14 crystals for one channel, complete instructions, and a 90 day parts and labor warranty. To order by mail, simply mail your check for $39.95 per unit (or $79.90 for two) plus $2.50 per order for postage, insurance and handling to the address shown below. (Illinois residents add 5% sales tax). But don't delay. It took only four advertisements last year to sell out our entire production.

The era of personal communications is the future of communications. Join the revolution. Order your PocketComs at no obligation today.

$39⁹⁵ NATIONAL INTRODUCTORY PRICE

JS&A NATIONAL SALES GROUP
Dept. SPG   JS&A Plaza
Northbrook, Illinois 60062
CALL TOLL-FREE . . 800 323-6400
In Illinois call . . . . (312) 498-6900
© JS&A Group, Inc., 1976

CASE 12

SIMPSON'S FOOD WAREHOUSE

VARIATION IN FOOD MERCHANDISING

Simpson's Food Warehouse is an experimental unit just opened by a major grocery store in the Southern California area. Basically, the operation is designed to allow members to buy food and items traditionally sold in supermarkets at reduced prices by cutting out many of the frills of regular grocery shopping, e.g., fancy displays, prepriced items, boxing of eggs, trimming of produce, bagging of purchases, etc. The objective is to provide lower prices by eliminating all store nonessentials and shifting to the customer certain tasks formerly performed by store personnel.

Operational Characteristics

Newspaper advertising began two weeks prior to the opening of Simpson's. The basic theme of the advertisements was simple and straightforward: "If you do not mind doing some of the work yourself and can stand the warehouse atmosphere, you can save a lot on those ever-increasing food bills." A brief description of how to shop at Simpson's was included in the advertisements (see Exhibit 12.1) along with a coupon for one month's free membership. Once store traffic is established and a large number of memberships have been issued, management plans to cut back on newspaper advertising and let "word of mouth" promotion take over.

Environmental Description

The store is located in a lower middle-class suburb, with almost direct access to a freeway. Within 10 minutes driving time are a high-income suburb, a poor inner-city district, and the city university community. The building is actually an old warehouse—in places there is no floor covering, only concrete. There are few merchandise displays. The interior has no ceiling, and the roof supports are visible. Items are stacked neatly in rows, and there are directional cards indicating where to look for a particular item.

The meat and produce departments are somewhat nicer in appearance—there is a tile floor and clean, well-maintained display cases. An effort is made to keep the store as clean as possible. The meat and produce departments are usually immaculate, but the rest of the store suffers from occasional untidiness (empty cartons disposed of in the aisles, etc.)

Present Situation

Simpson's has now been open for two months and management is concerned about the limited response which consumers have shown toward the store. Certain complaints have been voiced by consumers including:

- ☐ "Why do I have to 'pay' to shop here?"
- ☐ "Why don't you have a greater selection of brands?"
- ☐ "Your prices are not any better than those of the other stores."
- ☐ "I don't like to have to mark my purchases. The checkout clerk always looks at the prices suspiciously. Don't they trust me?"

Check out personnel have been instructed to spot check customer marked items against an up-to-date master price list because some people had been making errors. Store management also explained that prices can be kept low by offering only a limited selection of brands, although the store will always endeavor to have the most popular national brands in stock. Private label brands are not being carried at the present time. Exhibit 12.2 shows the results of a study comparing the prices of items in the Standard American Food Basket at Simpson's and three of its major competitors.

EXHIBIT 12.1
Description of Approach to Shopping at Simpson's Food Warehouse

1. A customer buys a membership card which is sold by the month or the year. The charge is 60 cents per month or $5.00 per year. If the customer feels after trying Simpson's Food Warehouse he or she is not realizing real savings, the membership card may be returned for a full refund.
2. Upon entering the store, the customer picks up a special marking pen. Items are stacked in open cases around the store; on each carton is marked a case price and a unit price. If the customer is buying an entire case, he or she simply transfers the case to the shopping cart, as it is already priced. If buying only an individual item, he or she marks the unit price on the item using the marking pen furnished, and proceeds.
3. Produce is selected and bagged by the customer, then taken to a Simpson's employee for weighing and pricing.
4. The store maintains a full service meat department. While custom-cut meats are available at discount prices, the greatest savings are realized by buying "family pack" meats. These are simply multiple packages; for example, each package containing two to four roasts instead of just one.
5. At the check-out, the customer places purchases on the counter where a Simpson's employee tallies them. Payment is by cash or check only, no credit cards are accepted. If a customer wishes to pay by check, a check-cashing identification card can be obtained at the store office. Customers bag their own groceries using bags or containers brought with them. If needed, bags are available at the store at a cost of 10 cents each.

EXHIBIT 12.2
Comparisons of Prices for Items in the Standard American Food Basket for Simpson's Food Warehouse and Three Major Competitors

	1	2	3	4
Coffee, Folgers 1-lb can	$1.75	$1.75	$1.75	$1.71
Soup, Campbell's chicken noodle 10 3/4 oz	.20	.21	.22	.20
Flour, Robin Hood 5 lb	.91	.87	.93	.95
Sugar, Domino 5 lb	1.29	1.29	1.25	1.05
Ground beef 1 lb	1.09	.75	.68	.69
Chicken, cut up, whole fryer 1 lb	.73	.71	.57	.68
Peanut butter, Jif 18 oz	.89	.89	.89	.87
Corn flakes, Kellogg's 12 oz	.45	.53	.53	67
Frozen corn, Birds Eye 10 oz	.45	.38	.43	.41
Detergent, Tide 49 oz	1.45	1.45	1.45	1.09
Toilet paper, Charmin 4 rolls	.71	.73	.73	.72
Potatoes, Idaho 5 lb	1.09	1.29	1.09	1.24
Milk, store brand, homogenized 1 qt	.43	.39	.45	.43
American cheese, Kraft 8 oz sliced	.89	.91	.91	.78
Eggs, medium 1 doz	.85	.89	.87	.83
Bread, Wonder enriched 20 oz	.59	.59	.57	.59
	$13.77	$13.63	$13.32	$12.91

Codes: 1—Local supermarket chain.
2—Discount supermarket.
3—National supermarket chain.
4—Simpson's food warehouse.

CASE 13

HYDE-PHILLIP CHEMICAL COMPANY
ALTERNATIVE FORMS OF SALES REPRESENTATION

Michael Claxton, a recent marketing graduate of a well-known college, has been assigned the task of evaluating Hyde-Phillip Chemical Company's methods of selling the firm's products. Hyde-Phillip currently utilizes a mix of company sales persons—merchant wholesalers and agent wholesalers—to present its products to present and potential users. While this combination of selling forces is somewhat unusual it reflects the orientation of management over time as to the relative values of alternative forms of sales representation. Claxton's challenge is to review the data that has been gathered on the three types of sales efforts, determine if additional information is needed, and make recommendations as to what changes, if any, should be made in the firm's approach to sales representation.

Information on the Company
Hyde-Phillip was formed in the early 1960's through the merger of Hyde Industrial Chemicals and Phillip Laboratories. Both firms had a broad range of experience in the development and production of certain types of chemi-

cals and related supplies for a variety of industrial·users. While the two firms had a few overlapping product lines, each brought to the merger some exclusive product offerings. The resulting combination of the two firms yielded a new organization capable of marketing a complete line of chemicals for industrial use.

Prior to the merger, Hyde Industrial Chemicals had utilized a group of industrial distributors (merchant wholesalers) to market its products. Phillip Laboratories, on the other hand, had several manufacturers' agents (agent wholesalers) who sold its product offering. The new firm, after the merger, retained some of the industrial distributors and some of the manufacturing agents and then began to develop its own sales force.

Today, Hyde-Phillip serves 30 sales territories in states east of the Mississippi through its own sales force of 50 individuals (six women and 44 men), nine industrial distributors, and nine manufacturers' agents. The 50 salespeople are about evenly allocated across twelve of the sales territories. Each of the industrial distributors and manufacturers' agents has exclusive selling rights in one of the 18 remaining sales territories. Individual distributors and agents have from five to 30 people working for them and many represent other noncompeting manufacturers. The 30 sales territories were originally established to represent areas of approximately equal sales potential for Hyde-Phillip's products.

Many types of sales support are made available to each sales territory by the company. Individual managers of the territories have the option of using or not using each type of sales support. Sales support items currently available include: (1) a variety of descriptive brochures to supplement the information given in the firm's product catalog, (2) study programs with cassette tapes to enable sales representatives to be more familiar with the firm's products and current market situations and developments, (3) a program to provide generous product samples to potential customers for test purposes, and (4) direct-mail programs aimed at prospective customers to solicit inquiries for descriptive materials and product samples.

Data on Sales Territories

As a first step in beginning his analysis, Claxton asked his assistant to compile the available information on each of the 30 sales territories. This information is presented in coded form in Exhibit 13.1.

In terms of level of sales, nine territories have annual sales in excess of $2 million, fifteen have sales between $1 and $2 million, and six have sales less than $1 million. As already indicated, in twelve of the territories the firm is represented by its own sales force, and industrial distributors and manufacturers' agents each represent the company in nine territories.

Based on estimates provided by the sales support department, twelve of the territories make extensive use of the available sales support programs, twelve are moderate users, and six are light users. Each of the firm's sales territories is also divided into one of three geographic divisions, Northern, Southern, or Eastern. As indicated in Exhibit 13.1, each of these geographic locations includes ten sales territories.

Initial Analysis

Using the information in Exhibit 13.1, Claxton constructed the cross tabulation of sales versus type of representation as shown in Exhibit 13.2. He first set up the cross tabulation using raw numbers and then calculated the conditional probabilities for each row and column.

As seen in part B of Exhibit 13.2, 30.0 percent of Hyde-Phillip's territories with sales over $2 million were ones served by industrial distributors. Only 11.1 percent of the largest sales territories were represented by manufacturers' agents and 33.3 percent were served by the company sales force. Stated differently, as shown in part C of Exhibit 13.2, 25.0 percent of territories served by the company's sales force had sales over $2 million, while 55.6 percent of the industrial distributors and 11.1 percent of the manufacturers' agents served territories with sales over $2 million.

Claxton's initial reaction was that the firm should consider replacing part of its own sales force and the manufacturers' agents with more industrial distributors. He was concerned, however, with what other variables should be taken into account to more fully analyze and evaluate Hyde-Phillip's current approach to sales representation.

EXHIBIT 13.1
Available Data on Sales Territories

TERRITORY NUMBER	LEVEL OF SALES	TYPE OF REPRESENTATION	USE OF SALES SUPPORT	GEOGRAPHIC LOCATION
1	2	1	2	3
2	3	1	3	3
3	2	2	1	1
4	1	1	1	1
5	2	3	1	1
6	2	1	2	1
7	3	3	2	3
8	1	2	1	1
9	2	1	2	2
10	2	1	2	3
11	1	2	1	1
12	1	1	1	2
13	2	2	2	2
14	2	3	2	1
15	1	1	2	3
16	2	3	2	2
17	2	1	3	1
18	1	2	1	2
19	2	3	2	2
20	3	1	3	2
21	1	3	1	3
22	2	2	1	3
23	3	3	1	1
24	3	1	3	2
25	3	2	3	1
26	1	2	1	2
27	2	1	2	2
28	1	2	1	3
29	2	3	3	3
30	2	3	2	3

Codes: Level of sales: 1 = over $2 million; 2 = $1–2 million; 3 = under $1 million.
Type of representation: 1 = company sales force; 2 = industrial distributor; 3 = manufacturers' agent.
Use of sales support: 1 = extensive user; 2 = moderate user; 3 = light user.
Geographic location: 1 = Northern; 2 = Southern; 3 = Eastern.

EXHIBIT 13.2
Cross Tabulation of Level of Sales Versus Type of Representation

		Company Salesforce (1)	Industrial Distributor (2)	Manufacturers' Agent (3)	Totals	
	Over $2 million (1)	3	5	1	9	
LEVEL OF SALES	$1–2 million (2)	6	3	6	15	A
	Under $1 million (3)	3	1	2	6	
	Totals	12	9	9		

		Company Salesforce (1)	Industrial Distributor (2)	Manufacturers' Agent (3)		
	Over $2 million (1)	33.3	55.6	11.1	100.0	
LEVEL OF SALES	$1–2 million (2)	40.0	20.0	40.0	100.0	B
	Under $1 million (3)	50.0	16.7	33.3	100.0	
	Totals	40.0	30.0	30.0	100.0	

		Company Salesforce (1)	Industrial Distributor (2)	Manufacturers' Agent (3)		
	Over $2 million (1)	25.0	55.6	11.1	30.0	
LEVEL OF SALES	$1–$2 million (2)	50.0	33.3	66.7	50.0	C
	Under $1 million (3)	25.0	11.1	22.2	20.0	
	Totals	100.0	100.0	100.0		

Code: A = raw numbers.
B = row conditional probabilities.
C = column conditional probabilities.

PART FIVE
PROMOTIONAL STRATEGY

CASE 14

YOUNGS DRUG PRODUCTS TROJAN CONDOMS

In late 1975, representatives of Youngs Drug Products and groups of other contraceptive manufacturers, planned-parenthood advocates, the clergy, and other interested parties met with the National Association of Broadcasters (NAB) to back a position paper prepared by them with the aid of the Population Institute of New York requesting a code change. The NAB turned down the request to allow the advertising of contraceptives on television but did agree to study the proposal and to entertain an appeal after six months.

The Company

Youngs Drug Products manufactures and distributes Trojan condoms and a variety of other items through drugstores. It is the endeavor of the company to develop, implement, and establish specific type products which would best fit in with a sales force contacting only pharmacies.

The firm's basis distribution policy is through registered wholesale drug houses who in turn sell to registered retail pharmacies. Over 75 percent of Youngs' business is done in this manner with the remainder of sales going direct to certain large and influential drug chains. Youngs' sales force, in excess of 100 people, contact the country's 47,000 drugstores on a planned frequency during the year. These salespeople write missionary orders which are turned over to the wholesaler for shipment. Sales of the firm's products are also made through additional sales forces working directly for the drug wholesalers.

The total market for condoms in the United States is estimated at approximately $147 million. Of the total about $70 million represents sales through pharmacies with the rest being marketed through vending machines, mail order, and mass merchandisers. Youngs is generally credited with having about 56 percent of those sales made through pharmacies.

The Advertising

Youngs originated consumer advertising for condoms in 1969 when the company decided it not only had a quality product to sell but a market that needed to know more about the product, both generically and brand specific. Use of the family planning aspects of condoms was not acceptable to most media, so the company decided to promote Trojans for their usefulness in preventing venereal disease. The first advertisements ran in *Sports* magazine with later ones in *Playboy, Family Health, Penthouse, Oui, Sexology,* and various other magazines.

After advertisements for male birth control devices were pretty well accepted by magazines the next logical marketing step seemed to be television commercials. To that end, two 30-second condom television spots were created and produced for Youngs and Poppe Tyson, the firm's advertising agency, by Trio Productions, Inc. For both commercials, the objective was to develop an institutional message in good taste—"one which would remind the viewer that condoms over the years have had a legitimate and helpful place in family planning." Exhibits 14.1 and 14.2 indicate the audio portions of the commercials along with artist renditions and verbal descriptions of the video portions.

With about 60 percent of the nation's television stations adhering to the NAB code, it was necessary to turn to noncode stations to carry the two commercials. During the last week in July 1975, station KNTV in San Jose, California agreed to run the commercials. The station first ran the commercials during an early evening movie rerun. The station's switchboard received a great many calls, mostly negative, and the commercials were dropped.

The press, however, got hold of the story making it a news item and the station decided to rerun one of the commercials as part of its news programming. When viewers' opinions were solicited the response was about 85 percent in favor of running the television spots. So the commercials went back on the air, this time on a late-hour slot, with little adverse viewer response. Several additional television stations agreed to run the commercials with generally acceptable viewer reaction. Radio commercials, using the audio portion of the television spots, were also accepted by several stations.

The Controversy

Reports that the Code Authority of the NAB was canvassing public opinion on the subject of changing its policy banning contraceptive advertising on television brought opposition to the change from several fronts, particularly the United States Catholic Conferences (USCC). In a statement calling for an end to contraceptive television commercials, Bishop James S. Rausch, general secretary of USCC, labeled such advertisements "a gross violation of the rights of parents to guide the moral and social development of their children."

With regard to restricting such advertisements to late evening hours he stated that "There is no acceptable compromise approach to this issue" because "recent studies of viewing habits show that many millions of children watch television after the so-called family viewing period." He added that "It would be unrealistic, unfair, and unacceptable to burden concerned parents with the task of monitoring the home television screen for commercial solicitations on behalf of contraceptives."

Fred Poppe, president of Poppe Tyson, in reply, said that viewer reaction to the Trojan commercials had run about twenty to one in favor of showing such advertisements. Based on viewer responses he indicated that there are three basic reasons that people support the advertisements:

1. They feel that the commercials should be allowed in deference to freedom of speech.
2. Viewers believe the advertisements are in good taste, often in better taste than other commercials and even the programs being offered.
3. They feel that with abortions and unwanted pregnancies becoming growing problems, people should be told about contraceptives.

In commenting on Trojan's media plan for 1976, Mr. Poppe stated, "We definitely will be using commercial television stations. We also definitely will be using Spanish radio and television along with a print schedule primarily in magazines." He also indicated that a number of radio stations, cable televison stations, UHF stations, and some outdoor media have expressed interest in running Youngs' advertisements.

AUDIO
Voice over: (Man)

To everything there is a season. And a time to every purpose under the heaven.

> . . . a time to weep.
> . . . a time to laugh.
> . . . a time to mourn
> . . . and a time to dance. [a]

The makers of Trojans Condoms believe there is a time for children. The right time. When they are wanted. And Trojans have helped people for over half a century safely practice responsible parenthood.

VIDEO

Young boy and girl running along the beach. We use slow motion, soft dissolves, facial closeups to establish a graphic poetic mood. Music over voices through to end when logo appears.

[a] *Quotation from Ecclesiastes III.*

EXHIBIT 14.2
"Cradle" 30-Second Spot Television Commercial for Youngs Drug Trojans

---

AUDIO
Voice over: (Tenderly)

People today know the importance of responsible parenthood . . . So they plan. Carefully. Thoughtfully. And with a great deal of love.

There is a time for having children. And when that time comes, nothing is more joyous.

The makers of Trojans Condoms have been helping people for over half a century safely practice responsible parenthood.

VIDEO
Open Tight on wooden pieces being glued and assembled. Soft lighting. Through a series of soft dissolves, we reveal that a cradle is being built by hand; we never see the person who is building it. Only the hands. Finally, we see a hand polishing one of the cradle rungs, then widen to see the cradle. A hand touches it and it begins to rock back and forth. Soft guitar instrumental over voice.

To logo.

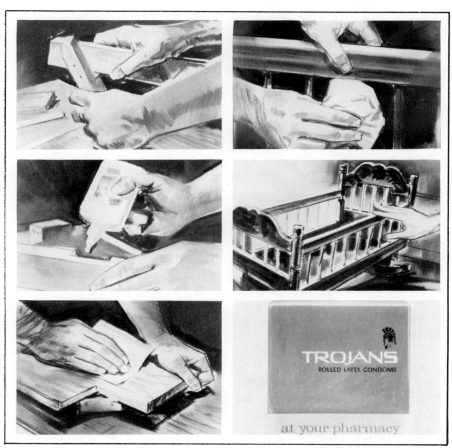

CASE 15

INTERNATIONAL TELEPHONE AND TELEGRAPH[1]
CORPORATE ADVERTISING

Not too many years ago I doubt that a talk on corporate advertising would have been sexy enough to hold the attention of a high-powered advertising agency meeting like this. Corporate advertising didn't have the appeal (or frankly, the budgets) of a new mouth wash, a new detergent, or a new refrigerator.

But of course, times change. Lately, vast new pressures have been directed against virtually all institutions—business organizations, included. Corporations have found it necessary to speak their piece to an often hostile community. Which is why you and I are here this morning, talking about this business of putting together a corporate advertising campaign.

But there's one difficulty we face in corporate advertising—and I'd like to address these remarks to it: How do we justify corporate advertising expenditures to a disciplined, bottom-line oriented management? With packaged goods or hard goods, you can follow Nielsens and factory sales. How

[1]Adapted from a talk given by John L. Lowden, Director, Advertising and Sales Promotion, International Telephone and Telegraph Corporation, at the 1975 Eastern Annual Conference of the American Association of Advertising Agencies.

do we prove the *tangible* returns of a corporate campaign, in the absence of such marketplace indicators? I offer the ITT campaign as an illustration of one way to go about it.

Motivation for the Campaign

To begin with, our current corporate campaign was a direct response to a need uncovered by research. I mentioned earlier the hostile climate that has beset corporations in the last few troubled years. At ITT, we were and are concerned about this antagonistic drift in public opinion, and so we asked the Yankelovich, Skelly & White organization to find out what people knew about our company.

This was in 1972; just three years ago. ITT was zooming to ninth largest industrial company in the Fortune 500—a major among majors. Yet, research found that most Americans knew very little about us. ITT was familiar to less than one out of three adult Americans in households with incomes of $15,000 or more. There was an extraordinary lack of knowledge about ITT—a vacuum being filled only by news stories reporting unfavorable allegations about us.

It wasn't a question of our not having advertised before. Through our corporate advertising agency—Needham, Harper & Steers—we had been running a successful print campaign for a number of years. But we had directed this effort at a narrow, carefully defined target group. We had aimed at people in business, finance, government, and the campus world . . . and we believed we were getting through.

What our research told us, unmistakably, was that this wasn't enough. It appeared that the so-called influentials weren't communicating downward, to others, such subjective reactions about ITT as awareness, understanding, and confidence. There were too many people out there—prosperous, relatively well-educated people—who didn't know *what* ITT was or did. They were voters, people who might be potential buyers of our stock, college students who are the influentials of tomorrow, and so on. The brute fact was, they didn't recognize our name as they would the familiar, consumer goods companies that some of you represent. And lacking knowledge about us, they were ready to believe anything said about us.

Communication Decisions

That is why we decided to shift most of our media dollars into television, taking our message to an audience a good deal larger than the audience we had been talking to.

There would still be a basic print schedule, directed at that part of the audience that watched little TV. But print's role was considered largely supportive of television.

Our job was to communicate how we could help improve the quality of life through the quality of our R&D, our products, our services. Television was a perfect vehicle for this—not only because it could help us demonstrate dramatically our concern and involvement, but because of its speed and efficiency in reaching the large audience we now had in mind.

Evaluative Marketing Research

Now, we knew that reaching this audience and changing minds in a relatively short time would be an expensive proposition. We also knew we had to demonstrate to our management (and to ourselves) that this expense was justified; that a major Corporate Advertising campaign, on the scale we projected, could fill the identity vacuum and dilute the unfavorable publicity we were getting. As I said, we had no Nielsens to go by; we had to create our own yardsticks.

So we undertook a major research program that had two key objectives:

1. To track changes in awareness, familiarity, and reputation of ITT among people in households with $15,000 plus annual incomes.
2. To assess the effectiveness of the campaign in improving attitudes among this target audience.

We developed a questionnaire, carefully pretested it, and then administered it, before the campaign began, to get a benchmark. Then we went back six months after . . . and again six months after that . . . and we are still continuing to chart our progress at six-month intervals.

The technical specifications called for a national probability sample of households having annual incomes of $15,000 or more. Each sampling has consisted of 1,500 or more telephone interviews.

The Campaign and Results

Let me show you some of our commercials now, beginning with the very first ITT corporate commercial that ever ran, and then some of the spots that followed. (See Exhibit 15.1.)

From the first, we felt we had an artistic success on our hands. Almost from the day these commercials started running, we heard good reports from people around the country. But even their enthusiasm didn't prepare us for the extraordinary improvement that research reported in our six-month checkups. Let me sketch the highlights.

Awareness and familiarity with ITT increased substantially—from 34 percent in January 1974 to 59 percent in July 1975.

The identity void is being filled on our terms. Awareness of ITT—*favorable* awareness—is now approaching that of other major corporations.

The effect of ITT's corporate television advertising on its corporate identity and reputation has been substantial . . . including its investment appeal.

Not only the association of ITT with these corporate strengths, but the actual changes have been impressive. For example:

- ☐ develops many new products, went from 46 percent in January 1974 to 70 percent in July 1975
- ☐ leader in technology, from 49 to 74 percent
- ☐ leads in R&D to improve products, from 46 to 68 percent
- ☐ makes quality products, from 54 to 77 percent
- ☐ reliable, from 48 to 65 percent

These increases relate directly to the subject matter of our commercials, but it's interesting to *note* some of the *implicit* messages that are getting through. Such as:

- ☐ cares about general public, from 31 to 43 percent
- ☐ protects jobs of U.S. workers, from 27 to 35 percent

And there were several other increments of particular note to our management:

- ☐ good stock to buy or own, from 52 to 65 percent
- ☐ good balance between profits and the public interest, from 29 to 36 percent

Summary Comments

There was much, much more in the way of gratifying results, including a firm vindication of our selection of TV as the primary medium for this effort. But perhaps I've already given you the flavor of the continuing success this campaign is enjoying.

Let me reiterate my opening question: can a corporate advertising campaign, particularly a rather substantial one, be justified to a financially disciplined management? In our experience, yes.

Skepticism toward business is a fact of our times, and certainly ITT has had more than its share of negative publicity. But a well-thought-out corporate campaign can go a long way toward countering a hostile press—and can be justified, to management, by carefully documented research.

EXHIBIT 15.1
Example Television Storyboards for ITT's Corporate Advertising Program

ITT

"Night Blindness" :60

PRODUCT: ITT NIGHT VISION SCOPE

GIRL: I'm going blind. The disease I have . . . something called Retinitis Pigmentosa . . .

is taking my sight away. Little by little, I can still see pretty well by day.

But in the dark, when you're still able to see things, the world to me looks . . .

like this . But there's a device that's being worked on that can help me.

You're looking through one now, just like the one I have. With this, I can see at night again. The people at ITT . . .

developed this device. They're working now with the Retinitis Pigmentosa Foundation

to make a smaller, less costly model for people like me. This new night vision device isn't available . . . yet.

But when it is there'll be some pretty grateful people. To you, this may seem ugly.

To me, it's beautiful.

ITT
**The best ideas are the
ideas that help people.**

EXHIBIT 15.1 (*Continued*)

ITT

"Heart Mannequin":60

PRODUCT: ELECTRONIC CIRCUITRY

SOUND EFFECTS: THROUGHOUT WE HEAR INTERWOVEN STRETCH-ES OF DOCTOR LECTURING, SOUNDS OF HEART BEATING.

ANNCR. (VOICE OVER): You're a student doctor. Your subject... heart disease.

How do you find a heart patient to study?

Well, one answer is Harvey...a mannequin with a heart.

Using Harvey, students can learn the signs and symptoms...for more kinds of heart disease than most doctors come across in a lifetime.

Doctors at the University of Miami Medical School developed this experimental mannequin.

The people at ITT designed its complex circuitry.

Now others are being built, with the same ITT circuitry, to help train tomorrow's doctors.

SOUND EFFECTS: HEARTBEAT BECOMES MORE PRONOUNCED BUILDING IN CRESCENDO.

ANNCR. (VOICE OVER): When you consider that heart disease is the nation's Number One killer, you can see where Harvey has quite a future.

ITT
The best ideas are the ideas that help people.

EXHIBIT 15.1 (*Continued*)

CASE 16
ALLEGHENY AIRLINES
IMAGE BUILDING ADVERTISING

During the week of May 17, 1976, Allegheny Airlines launched a major new marketing campaign, including widespread advertising built on the theme, "It Takes A Big Airline . . . It Takes Allegheny." The theme was chosen after research conducted by the J. Walter Thompson Co., Allegheny's new advertising agency, showed that public impression of an airline is heavily influenced by perceived size of the airline.

"We found that 'big is better' in public perception of airlines," stated Harry T. Chandis, Allegheny's vice-president of marketing. "We also found that Allegheny is misperceived by a large percentage of the public as being a small airline, when in fact this is not true by any measurement."

Company Background
Allegheny Airlines, Inc., was organized March 5, 1937 under the laws of the states and two Canadian provinces. The firm is North America's sixth international scheduled air transportation of passengers, property, and mail. The company merged with Lake Central Airlines in 1968 and Mohawk Airlines in 1972.

Today, Allegheny provides services to more than 100 cities in eighteen states and two Canadian providences. The firm is North America's sixth largest passenger-carrying airline. Its operations are subjected to the jurisdiction of the Civil Aeronautics Board which regulates the routes that may be flown and the fares that may be charged. Exhibit 16.1 indicates Allegheny's 1975 route system and Exhibit 16.2 presents selected operating statistics for 1971 through 1975.

1975 Marketing Efforts

Allegheny's 1975 advertising and sales effort featured a new aircraft color design and a new corporate identity—"a symbol of our dedication to provide the best for our customers"—and a radio and newspaper campaign featuring employees and customers. Advertisements proclaimed "the more than 7,000 Allegheny people living and working alongside you . . . are professional people—ready to give their best all the time—everytime." Also pledged were convenient schedules at lowest possible fares and the latest in (automatic) ticketing, reservations, and terminal facilities.

Allegheny introduced two unique discounts to attract more pleasure and personal travel during 1975. One plan, the Group 4–9 Fare, featured 20 percent discounts on roundtrip air fares for groups of at least four but no more than nine persons. The Liberty Fare, as shown in an advertisement in Exhibit 16.3, offered three unlimited travel plans—7 days for $129, 14 days for $149, or 21 days for $179. The president of the American Society of Travel Agents cited the Liberty Fare as an "innovative new approach" to the discretionary travel market.

A marketing survey in the fall of 1975, however, showed that most of Allegheny's customers were business travelers. Less than 30 percent were traveling on vacations or personal/pleasure trips.

A Marketing Opportunity

According to a recent study conducted for Allegheny, a total of 49 percent of the respondents who had not flown the airline rated it overall as only poor or fair. Specifically, these respondents rated the firm down in such areas as experienced pilots, safety, maintenance, and dependability. Those respondents who had flown with Allegheny did rate it much higher, however. The research also revealed that Allegheny was more likely to be compared with Piedmont Airlines (a much smaller, regional carrier) than with such airlines as American, Trans World, and United. Based on the research results, it seemed that Allegheny was still suffering a poor public image stemming from the days when it was primarily a commuter carrier.

The Image Changing Campaign

As indicated at the outset, Allegheny began a new advertising campaign in May 1976, designed to compare and associate itself with the major air carriers. Allegheny's size is illustrated to the public through advertising messages such as:

- ☐ "It Takes a Big Airline to Fly Over a Million More Passengers a Year than Pan Am."
- ☐ "It Takes a Big Airline to Operate More Daily Flights than TWA."
- ☐ "It Takes a Big Airline to Fly to More American Cities than American."
- ☐ "It Takes a Big Airline to Operate One of the World's Largest Jet Fleets."

The introductory advertisements for print media feature Allegheny employees. An example print advertisement for this phase of the campaign is shown in Exhibit 16.4. Follow-up commercials and print advertisements show Ben Franklin and George Washington touring the original Colonies in an Allegheny airplane.

Allegheny is also changing its media mix with increased emphasis on television. About 45 percent of the firm's 1976 advertising budget of $5.2 million is being devoted to spot television in twenty markets. A major increase in the use of magazines is also taking place. Some 28 percent of the budget is being allocated to regional editions of such magazines as *Time, Newsweek, U.S. News & World Report,* and *Sports Illustrated.* Newspapers are receiving 20 percent of the advertising while radio and billboards account for the remainder of the funds.

Mr. Chandis admits that Allegheny has a major task in attempting to change its image. He explains, however, that the short-run objective is to make Allegheny a more acceptable alternative compared to its competitors. The longer term goal is to give Allegheny a distinctive identity and to make it a preferred choice among air travelers.

EXHIBIT 16.1
Allegheny Airlines 1975 Route System

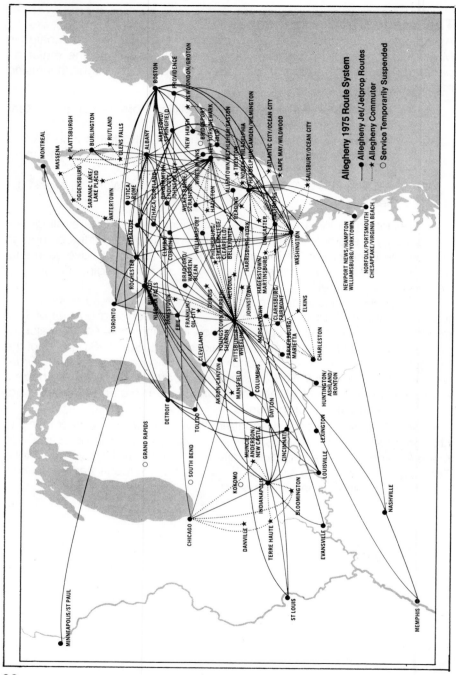

EXHIBIT 16.2
Allegheny Airlines, Inc.
Selected Operating Statistics
(Five years ended December 31, 1975)

	1975	1974	1973	1972	1971
Revenue plane miles flown (000)	70,005	75,690	84,917	72,550	53,327
Revenue passengers (000)	10,297	10,909	10,840	9,371	6,490
Available seat miles (000)	6,203,024	6,444,146	6,819,835	5,667,301	4,310,147
Revenue passenger miles flown (000)	3,304,490	3,414,912	3,302,003	2,770,787	1,895,037
Passenger load factor	53.3%	53.0%	48.4%	48.9%	44.0%
Operating breakeven passenger load factor (without subsidy)	52.8%	50.3%	45.9%	46.2%	42.6%
Passenger revenue per revenue passenger mile flown	10.42¢	9.86¢	8.96¢	8.76¢	8.61¢
Available ton miles flown (000)	758,076	786,581	832,488	701,225	550,759
Revenue ton miles flown (000)	363,237	380,067	375,087	311,924	213,349
Cargo ton miles flown (000)	32,787	38,575	44,888	34,845	23,829
Cost per available ton mile	48.8¢	44.5¢	37.1¢	35.7¢	31.2¢
Cost per available seat mile	5.96¢	5.43¢	4.52¢	4.42¢	3.99¢
Cost per revenue ton mile	101.8¢	92.1¢	82.2¢	80.2¢	80.6¢
Cost per revenue passenger mile	11.19¢	10.25¢	9.34¢	9.03¢	9.07¢
Average passenger journey (miles)	318.7	312.3	304.1	295.5	291.0
Number of employees	7,329	7,995	7,700	7,490	4,928
Aircraft in service	83	101	108	102	72
Total operating revenues (000)	$373,106	$ 368,547	$ 328,501	$ 267,718	$ 178,344
Net Income (loss) (000)	$ (9,898)	$ 6,024	$ 6,212	$ 6,068	$ (1,571)

EXHIBIT 16.3
Description of Allegheny's 1975 Liberty Fare

Allegheny announces unlimited air travel at one low price.

7 days for $129
14 days for $149
21 days for $179

It's an Allegheny exclusive. Unlimited air travel anywhere we fly, except Canada, for one, low price with your choice of plans.

And it's easy to use because there are just three basic rules:

1. Purchase your Liberty Fare exchange order 7 days before you want to take off. Make your reservations anytime.

2. Depart before noon on weekdays or anytime on a weekend—and plan to spend at least 3 full days away.

3. You can visit as many Allegheny cities in the U.S. as you wish, buy only one stopover per city is allowed —as long as you don't return to your originating city for a stopover. A connection through a city doesn't count as a stopover.

And there's more good news. Children, 2-11, fly for half the fare when accompanied by at least one adult. That makes their ticket—for a whole week—less than $65.

So, look at our map, pick the places you want to go—then see your Travel Agent or give Allegheny a call for complete details. We'll show you how to plan a super vacation with fly/drive and tour packages to get the most for your money with our new Liberty Fare. Or with any one of our other value-packed USAir fares. Fares quoted above include taxes. Nominal security surcharge extra.

Use our Liberty Fare and the sky's the limit.

PART SIX
PRICING STRATEGY

CASE 17

TULLER FRUIT FARM (B)[1]
PRICING FRESH ORANGE JUICE

As indicated in Tuller Fruit Farm (A) Charles Tuller and his family have successfully operated a roadside marketing facility for over fifteen years. The business offers consumers many country fresh products and produce items including cider, donuts, peanut butter, apples, sweet corn, pumpkins, etc.

One of the products Tuller's sells is fresh orange juice. The following comments were made about this product by Charles Tuller in connection with a seminar on his firm's operations.

"We also have an orange juice machine. We've had it just about a year, and have run about 800 boxes of oranges through. We sell it for $4 a gallon, or $1.25 a quart. I can't get half-gallon jugs, so we've never put a price on it. It's not a real fancy machine, but it does the trick. It cuts the orange in half, wrings it, and diposes of it underneath in a trash receptacle. You can do a gallon in a couple of minutes."

[1]Study of this case should include a careful review of Tuller Fruit Farm (A). Portions of this case were adapted from a talk given by Charles Tuller at the Fourteenth Annual Ohio Roadside Marketing Conference, January 6–8, 1974, sponsored by the Department of Agricultural Economics and Rural Sociology, The Ohio State University and The Ohio Cooperative Extension Service.

"If any of you are interested in this (as I was), no one could tell me what the yield was on a box of oranges. Now, I know some of you would like to know. It is 2 gallons, and the only way to get any more out of it is to add water. Make sure, above all, that you warm those oranges first—set them out at room temperature for a couple of days. The colder they are, the less juice. If you've got time to roll them, that helps. Don't bottle ahead. A lot of guys will bottle up and set it in the case; it separates. We do ours as they wait; that is what they want."

"We sell it at 20 cents for an 8-ounce glass and 30 cents for a 12-ounce. We are paying $3.75 at the terminal for oranges—this is a good little investment. I think it's $825 for the machine itself; jugs are 8 to 10 cents. Works out real good."

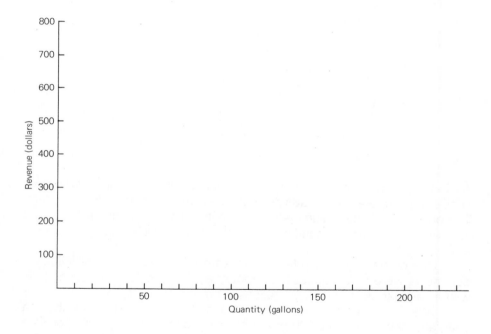

CASE 18

JAI LAI RESTAURANT

REBATE PRICE PROMOTIONS

The Jai Lai Restaurant is a large, high-quality, "cloth tablecloth and nap-kins" establishment. Its colorful history dates back to 1933, when Jasper E. Wottring founded the original cafe. He conceived the name from the game Jai Alai, which he observed being played while visiting Florida. The "A" was removed from Alai in the belief it would make the name easier to recognize and remember.

In the early fifties the Jai Lai was moved to a new building with a seating capacity of 600. The large dining area was separated into five rooms by Spanish style open arches, and the interior included such interesting touches as a large bar dating back to pre-prohibition days and exotic fish in lighted aquariums mounted in the perimeter walls.

The present owner and president of the corporation, Ted Girves, bought out one of the partners in 1963 and became a 50 percent stockhol-der. Mr. Wottring had died in the late 1950's. His son Dave is general manager. This new management team has been responsible for several changes, including hiring more waitresses instead of waiters and expanding the menu.

Slow Business During the Week

In early 1975, management decided to tackle a problem which seems to plague the restaurant business in general—how to generate more business on the slow weekdays (Monday–Thursday). The Jai Lai had no trouble drawing turn-away crowds on the weekends, yet weekday patronage was disappointing. Whereas they would typically serve 1200–1300 people on Saturday night, the average Monday crowd would total only 350–400 people.

Management examined certain approaches, such as outright discounting and coupons, which had been adopted by competitors, and concluded that such programs might harm the restaurant's quality image and convey the impression that they were "hurting" for business. Any program they adopted would have to be distinctive and effective, yet not jeopardize the quality image they had worked so long and hard to achieve.

Proposal—A Rebate Program

The automotive rebate programs then in progress inspired the idea of a similar "rebate" on selected dinners. Customers purchasing the selected dinners on Monday through Thursday evenings would receive the rebate in the form of silver dollars at the time the bill was paid.

There was a certain logic behind the rebate format:

- ☐ A silver dollar rebate, as opposed to a simple discount or paper-money rebate, would be much more distinctive, stimulating conversation and recall.
- ☐ While other programs such as coupons or discounts actually reduced the amount of the bill and thus tended to reduce tip income and hurt employee morale, a rebate would have but a limited effect in this direction.
- ☐ Management could vary the dinners eligible for rebate and observe the resulting customer behavior.

It was decided that the program would have the following objectives:

1. to better utilize the restaurant's capacity during the week
2. to increase profitability[1]
3. to broaden its customer base, i.e., to attract new, regular customers.

The last objective was considered particularly important. The management felt that even if the restaurant only broke even on the incremental

---

[1]In order to increase profitability, there would have to be a substantial sales increase of relatively expensive dinners. Jai Lai's total direct costs amounted to about 67–75 percent of the menu price, with 40–50 percent being direct food costs and 27–30 percent being direct labor costs.

weekday business, the program would still be worthwhile if it attracted new, regular clientele. Such people might return on a weekend or on a weekday (ordering a dinner not eligible for rebate) and thus improve overall profitability. The management felt particularly confident that the restaurant's quality food and atmosphere would induce many of the first-time visitors to return.

Implementation of the Program

The rebate program was initiated in early March, coupled with Sunday newspaper advertising to build awareness of the program. Examples of the newspaper advertising are shown in Exhibit 18.1.

The effect of the rebate program was immediate and dramatic, the customer "head count" from Monday to Thursday, which had been showing a decrease in January and February compared with the same period of the pervious year, began to increase. Number of customers for the weekend, however, seemed to be relatively unaffected. Head count statistics, which include both lunch and dinner, for the first five months of 1975 are presented in Exhibit 18.2.

While lunches remained about constant, the number of weekday dinners served increased dramatically. Virtually the total increase, however, could be attributed to the rebate items as shown in Exhibit 18.3.

Although dollar value per check decreased slightly, revenue overall rose substantially. The restaurant was able to handle the increased number of patrons with only a 20 percent increase in the weekday work force. Three productivity ratios, as presented in Exhibit 18.4, showed positive trends.

Review of the Program

Management, although encouraged by the response to the rebate program, had several misgivings at the end of the program's first three months. First, weekend business had hardly been affected by the program. Second, management had noted that as soon as a dinner was no longer eligible for rebate, its sales immediately plummeted to pre-rebate levels. (Of course, sales of dinners newly placed on rebate immediately rose.) Third, the incremental sales of a dinner placed on rebate seemed to be greatly affected by the original price of the dinner.

Inexpensive dinners placed on rebate suddenly became extremely popular, whereas expensive dinners experienced relatively modest increases. The Club Steak Dinner ($4.95) went from average Monday–Thursday sales of 45 weekly to 600–700 weekly within two weeks of being made eligible for rebate. After four weeks the Porterhouse Steak Dinner ($8.50) replaced the Club Steak dinner on the list of eligible rebate dinners. The result, Club Steak sales immediately slipped to Monday–Thursday sales of 50 weekly; Porterhouse sales increased, but not so dramatically—from Monday–Thursday sales of 20 weekly to about 210 weekly.

In conclusion, management began to view their new Monday–Thursday trade not as new regular customers, but more as bargain-hunting "opportunists" who would not patronize the restaurant except as induced by the rebate. At this point in time they are trying to evaluate the merits of continuing the rebate program.

EXHIBIT 18.1
Examples of Newspaper Adertisements for Rebate Program

**Get back 2 Silver Dollars...
...and enjoy a great dinner, too!**

Enjoy one of our weekly featured dinners at our regular menu price and get back two silver dollars as a cash rebate. This offer applies on Mondays through Thursdays only. Here are this week's special features:

- **Roast Prime Rib of Beef**
  (Menu price $7.50)
- **U.S. PRIME N.Y. Cut Steak**
  (Menu price $8.75)
- **Broiled Florida Red Snapper**
  (Menu price $6.25)

Jai Lai dinners include relish dish, salad, potato, vegetable, our own fresh-baked rolls and herb butter.

The Jai Lai *Restaurant*

1421 Olentangy River Road at West Fifth Avenue. Phone 421-7337
11 a.m. to 1 a.m. daily. 11 a.m. to 9 p.m. Sundays and holidays.
Fiesta Cocktail Hours: 2 to 6:30 p.m.

**Get back 2 Silver Dollars...
...and enjoy a great dinner, too!**

Enjoy one of our weekly featured dinners at our regular menu price and get back two silver dollars as a cash rebate. This offer applies on Mondays through Thursdays only. Here are this week's special features:

- **Our famous Prime Rib Dinner**
  (Menu price $6.95)
- **Broiled Lake Superior Jumbo White Fish**
  (Menu price $4.25)
- **Chopped Round Steak**
  (Menu price $4.25)

Jai Lai dinners include relish dish, salad, potato, vegetable, our own fresh-baked rolls and herb butter.

The Jai Lai *Restaurant*

1421 Olentangy River Road at West Fifth Avenue. Phone 421-7337
11 a.m. to 1 a.m. daily. 11 a.m. to 9 p.m. Sundays and holidays.
Fiesta Cocktail Hours: 2 to 6:30 p.m.

EXHIBIT 18.2
Head Count Statistics, 1974 and 1975

WEEK ENDING	1975		1974	
	M-T-W-T	F-S-S	M-T-W-T	F-S-S
1-12	3,899	3,706	4,265	3,642
1-19	4,683	3,340	4,774	4,609
1-26	4,518	3,843	4,323	4,595
2-2	4,427	4,230	5,014	4,176
2-9	4,090	3,887	4,054	4,428
2-16	4,079	4,604	5,678	4,679
2-23	4,252	3,762	4,787	3,933
3-2	3,830	3,930	4,832	4,420
3-9 [a]	3,911	4,080	4,092	4,286
3-16	6,071	4,419	4,843	4,651
3-23	6,848	4,730	4,915	5,083
3-30	5,964	4,744	4,749	4,818
4-6	5,143	3,871	4,346	4,437
4-13	4,877	3,859	4,561	5,319
4-20	5,745	3,955	4,507	4,274
4-27	6,192	4,672	5,076	4,862
5-4	6,386	4,353	4,737	4,650
5-11	6,345	5,882	5,170	6,408
5-18	6,068	4,255	4,826	4,418
5-25	5,990	3,662	5,194	4,179

[a] Rebate instated.

EXHIBIT 18.3
Number of Rebate and Nonrebate Dinners and Totals
(First Five Months of 1975, Mondays Through Thursdays Only)

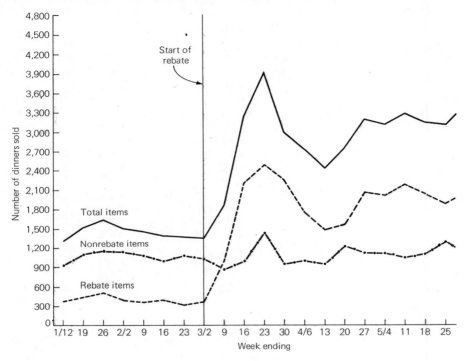

EXHIBIT 18.4
Changes in Selected Productivity Ratios

	PREREBATE JAN–FEB 1975	REBATE PERIOD MAR–MAY 1975
Average customers served/Man-hour	1.34	1.49
Average dollar volume/Man-hour	$8.09	$8.72
Average labor cost on a percent of sales	30.4%	28.5%

CASE 19

HAIRE BROTHERS FUNERAL CHAPEL

PRICING FUNERAL SERVICES

Ever since the firm's founding in 1895, Haire Brothers Funeral Chapel has used what is known as the unit pricing system. Under this approach to pricing the consumer is quoted a single price which includes the funeral director's professional service, the use of the firm's physical facilities and automotive equipment, and a casket. Roger Haire, manager of the firm and grandson of one of the founders, is concerned about whether or not it is time to change to another method of quoting funeral services.

Current Approach to Pricing

As indicated, Haire Brothers uses the unit approach to pricing. Prices for a complete funeral are established by applying a multiplier to the wholesale cost of the casket. The multiplier varies from 5.2 down to 3.2 with the higher values being applied to the lower cost caskets. This approach to pricing yields a range of complete funeral services priced from $468 to $3,520.

In reviewing other possible approaches to quoting price, Roger compiled the following information on the three most widely used methods[1]:

[1]Portions of these descriptions are adapted from a study done by the Batesville Casket Company entitled, "Funeral Directors' Pricing Methods, A Comprehensive National Survey," 1968.

UNIT

One price covers all the costs of the funeral except cash advances and optional extras. This is the most widely used method at the present time and is frequently based on some multiple times the funeral director's cost of the casket. Some funeral homes vary the value of the multiple, using a higher multiple for lower cost caskets than for more expensive ones. Other funeral directors compute their overhead structure and add this to a reasonable markup on a given casket to arrive at the total unit price.

The unit price usually includes such items as:

1. removal of remains to mortuary
2. complete preparation and dressing of remains
3. securing of necessary certificates and permits
4. use of mortuary facilities
5. assistance of the mortuary staff
6. transportation of the remains to the cemetery
7. fixed amount of additional transportation to cemetery
8. acknowledgment cards and memorial register
9. casket selected

COMPLETE ITEMIZED

This method goes to the other extreme in breaking out a separate price for each element of the funeral service. Certain states have passed legislation requiring all funeral homes to use this pricing method. The logic is that if consumers know what they are paying for, they will be better able to select exactly what they need and want.

The complete itemized method provides a separate price for each of the following:

1. removal of remains
2. embalming
3. dressing, casketing, and cosmetizing
4. use of chapel
5. use of other mortuary facilities and equipment
6. staff assistance
7. funeral coach
8. additional vehicles
9. casket
10. memorial register
11. acknowledgment cards
12. usually continues on with all other items that are considered as extras in all others' pricing methods

PROFESSIONAL

The professional pricing system, sometimes called the functional approach, has a separate fee for the professional services of the funeral director rather than just including them with the merchandise he sells. Under the professional system, the funeral director charges for his services in the same manner as a doctor or lawyer. The casket is then sold separately with a normal markup.

Two to five separate categories may be used with this method. Together they cover the cost of the funeral except any cash advances or optional extras. Various categories that may be used in different combinations are:

1. professional services
2. preparation for burial
3. use of facilities and equipment
4. motor vehicles
5. cost of the casket

Possible Need for Change

Based on a national sample of 1,060 respondents a recent marketing research study found that the majority of consumers indicate a preference for more information concerning funeral prices.[2] When offered a choice of the three common methods of pricing funerals, 33.3 percent stated a preference for unit pricing, 16.5 percent preferred professional pricing, and 50.2 percent voiced a preference for itemized pricing. These responses seem consistent with public reaction today under the concept of consumerism, specifically in the area of having more information available to the consumer.

In August 1975 the Federal Trade Commission issued a series of proposed rules for the funeral industry including a specific approach to price disclosures. While it may be some time before a final decision is made regarding the proposed rules by the federal government, certain states have already enacted legislation which specifies that funeral directors must disclose more price information in their dealings with consumers.

The specific language of the FTC regarding the price list is as follows:

> In connection with the sale or offering for sale of funeral services and/or merchandise to the public, in or affecting commerce as "commerce" is defined in the Federal Trade Commission Act, it is an unfair or deceptive act or practice for any funeral service industry member: To fail to furnish to each customer who inquires in person about the arrangement, purchase, and/or prices of

[2]From Roger D. Blackwell and W. Wayne Talarzyk, *American Attitudes Toward Death and Funeral Service*. Evanston, Illinois: The Casket Manufacturers Association, 1974.

funeral goods or services, prior to any agreement on such arrangement or selection by the customer or to any customer who by telephone or letter requests written price information, a printed or typewritten price list, which the customer may retain, containing the prices (either the retail charge or the price per hour, mile or other unit of computation) for at least each of the following items:

(i) Transfer of remains to funeral home.

(ii) Embalming.

(iii) Use of facilities for viewing.

(iv) Use of facilities for funeral service.

(v) Casket (a notation that a separate casket price list will be provided before any sales presentation for caskets is made).

(vi) Hearse.

(vii) Limousine.

(viii) Services of funeral director and staff.

(ix) Outer interment receptacles (if outer interment receptacles are sold, a notation that a separate outer interment receptacle price list will be provided before any sales presentation for such items is made).[3]

ROI Approach to Pricing

In his research on pricing, Roger also reviewed a working paper by Roger D. Blackwell, W. Wayne Talarzyk, and David C. Beever entitled, *The Return-On-Investment Approach to Professional Funeral Pricing.* The authors suggested that regardless of the method of *price quotation* (unit, itemized, or professional) a funeral director's approach to *price determination* should take into account a fair return-on-investment.

The following sections indicate the four basic stages involved in implementing an ROI pricing system[4]:

Stage 1—Determining Fixed and Variable Expenses

The first stage in applying ROI procedures to pricing is a determination of fixed and variable expenses of the funeral firm. This determination should be based upon accurate information in as detailed form as possible. A lack of detailed accounting information concerning fixed and variable costs is not the obstacle that might be assumed. It is probable that most funeral firm managers, because of the personal nature and size of the firm, can make usable estimates of the proportion of costs which are fixed and variable. As use of the system develops, based upon the preliminary estimates by management, the accounting system can gradually be modified as appropriate to provide more refined information concerning fixed and variable costs.

[3]Extracted from the *Federal Register,* Vol. 40, No. 169, Friday, August 29, 1975, p. 39903.

[4]From Roger D. Blackwell, W. Wayne Talarzyk, and David C. Beever, *The Return-On-Investment Approach to Professional Funeral Pricing,* Columbus, Ohio; New Horizons Publishing, Inc., 1976.

Stage 2—Programming Desired Profitability

The programmed profit is then added to the fixed costs of the firm, to be recovered from the sales of service and merchandise. Frequently, pricing systems currently used by funeral firms fail to include the "expense" of capital in the calculation of total fixed costs, thus understating true "overhead" of the funeral firm.

Stage 3—Determining Merchandise Contribution

The third stage in ROI pricing is the determination of contribution to overhead to be derived from the sale of merchandise. In addition to cover the wholesale cost of the merchandise (such as caskets, vaults and clothing) the merchandise will normally be priced to contribute some amount to the overhead that must be recovered from each family served. For example, if a firm's average merchandise sale was $600 and the average wholesale cost of that merchandise was $300, an average contribution of $300 per family would be derived from the sale of merchandise.

The pricing methods currently used in the funeral service field frequently fail to deduct the contribution of merchandise from the overhead of the firm. Unless the merchandise is sold at cost, however, a contribution is made to the overhead of the firm and should be subtracted from the amount to be recovered in the prices for services and facilities.

Stage 4—Determining Prices for Services and Facilities

The fourth stage in ROI pricing is to allocate the remainder of overhead costs from Stage 3 and the variable costs to services and facilities provided to families. The allocation should be based upon the costs associated with each component, moderated by the relative values perceived by consumers.

The fourth stage may be extended to three forms, influenced by the final method of price quotation to be used.

a. *Unit Pricing*—The total amount from Stage 3 still to be recovered is divided by the anticipated number of standard services to yield the price charged to consumers for services and facilities. To this amount is added variable costs and the casket charge to yield the total unit price.
b. *Functional Pricing*—The total amount from Stage 3 still to be recovered is allocated to the major functions to be performed. After this allocation the total amount of costs for each function is divided by the anticipated number of times that function is to be performed. To this amount is added the variable costs for each function to yield to price to be quoted to the consumer.
c. *Itemized Pricing*—The process described for functional pricing is repeated, except that the allocation is performed for each component which is to be itemized in the price quotation to the consumer.

Financial Data

Roger decided that it would be appropriate for him to at least work through the basics of the ROI approach to pricing before deciding whether or not to change his method of price quotation. To that end he began to assemble the necessary financial data to implement the ROI system. Exhibits 19.1 and 19.2 are the firm's most recent balance sheet and income statement, respectively.

In analyzing the operating expenses for 1976, Roger determined that about $148,000 represented fixed expenses with the remaining $14,738 being variable. Based on 160 families served during 1976 the variable costs per case then came out to be $92.

Roger was somewhat uncertain as to what would be the appropriate rate of return-on-investment for his funeral home. He also wondered what markup should be used for such merchandise items as caskets, vaults, and clothing. He did ascertain that while not all families purchased all three types of merchandise, the "average" family during 1976 purchased merchandise items with the following wholesale costs: caskets—$197; vaults—$85; clothing—$10.

EXHIBIT 19.1
Balance Sheet for Haire Brothers Funeral Chapel
(December 31, 1976)

ASSETS			
Current Assets			
Cash (or equivalent)	9,312		
Accounts receivable	27,480		
Inventory	19,671		
Other	759		
Total		57,222	
Fixed Assets			
Physical facilities	180,485		
Less accumulated depreciation	(55,705)	124,780	
Automotive	29,719		
Less accumulated depreciation	(13,507)	16,212	
Total		140,992	
Total Assets			198,214

LIABILITIES AND OWNER'S EQUITY			
Current Liabilities			
Accounts payable	10,473		
Notes payable	18,683		
Other	7,512		
Total		36,668	
Long-term Liabilities		69,950	
Total Liabilities		106,618	
Owner's Equity (Net Worth)		91,596	
Total Liabilities and Owner'sEquity			198,214

EXHIBIT 19.2
Income Statement for Haire Brothers Funeral Chapel
(Year Ending December 31, 1976)

Sales	$221,781
Cost of merchandise	46,752
Gross margin	175,029
Operating expenses	162,738
Net profit (before taxes)	12,291
Taxes	3,872
Net profit (after taxes)	$ 8,419

PART SEVEN
EMERGING DIMENSIONS

CASE 20

CAMPUS CRUSADE FOR CHRIST INTERNATIONAL HERE'S LIFE, AMERICA CAMPAIGN

Anyone spending time in Atlanta during the spring of 1975 would remember well the words, "I found it." For three weeks in May the slogan was everywhere: on billboards, television screens, radios, in newspapers, and even on lapel buttons and bumper stickers. More than 10,000 people phoned an advertised number, giving their names and addresses so they could discover exactly what had been found. Also over one-half of the telephone households in the city were phoned by workers explaining "how to find it." The campaign was part of the Here's Life, America strategy—a plan developed and coordinated by Campus Crusade for Christ to expose the metropolitan areas in Canada and the United States to the gospel of Jesus Christ.

History of Campus Crusade

Campus Crusade began as an interdenominational student Christian movement on the campus of the University of California at Los Angeles in the fall of 1951 when Bill Bright and his wife Vonette leased a home near the campus and began to tell students about Jesus Christ. A 24-hour chain of prayer was organized, and teams of students were trained to take the gospel into fraternities, sororities, and residence halls. Approximately 250 students committed their lives to Christ during that first year.

Soon laymen began to ask for the same training that staff and students were receiving. From this, and through the mass media, grew outreaches to laymen, high school students, and military personnel throughout the world. With a staff of more than 5,000, Campus Crusade for Christ now has an active ministry on hundreds of United States campuses and in more than half of the major countries of the world.

Campus Crusade is not an organization that solicits membership in the usual sense of the word. Instead, it is a voluntary movement of individuals who agree with its objectives and methods. As such, it represents no particular denomination, but seeks to serve as an evangelistic arm of the church. All of the staff members must raise their own financial support, and there is no financial backing from any source other than voluntary donations.

Objectives of Campus Crusade

From its beginning, Campus Crusade has embraced the historical Christian position that changing a world must first involve changing the hearts, minds, and lives of people. Racism, violence, crime, immorality, and other problems, according to this point of view, are symptoms of the basic fact that man is inherently self-centered and separated from God. This separation is the result of sin; matters will not change unless man accepts the free gift of love and forgiveness offered by Jesus Christ.

Therefore, the basic purpose of the movement is to change the world through "spiritual revolution" in obedience to Christ's command that His message of love and forgiveness should be taken to all corners of the earth. This command is referred to as the Great Commission, and it is the goal of Campus Crusade to help fulfill this Commission in this generation.

Purpose of Here's Life, America

Here's Life, America, a movement comprised of cooperating local churches, has set as its goal, ". . . to help reach the entire nation with the message of new life in Jesus Christ by the end of 1976." Its purpose is to create an environment in each city that will bring trained Christians from participating churches together with individuals desiring to know more about a personal relationship with Jesus Christ.

Undergirding the campaign in each city is a network of churches representing numerous denominations. The following information, extracted from a mailing designed to encourage churches to participate in the campaign, indicates some of the possible benefits for individual churches.

"Here's how your church will benefit:

- ☐ Renewed vision and increased excitement among your church members.
- ☐ Training for your members in how to experience the abundant Christian life and how to share their faith.
- ☐ The names of people from your area who respond to the media campaign asking to know more about Christ.
- ☐ Growth in your church from enrollment of new Christians and other interested individuals in follow-up Bible study classes.
- ☐ An opportunity to begin an on-going movement of discipleship and evangelism in your church that will have a continuing impact upon your community."

Overview of the Campaign

A basic overview of the total campaign is shown in Exhibit 20.1. As indicated in this exhibit, several weeks prior to the use of mass media and telephone, volunteers learned how to communicate their faith in Christ and how to teach the basics of the Christian life to those who will respond to the campaign. Exhibit 20.2 presents a flyer used to invite interested people to this training institute.

Two basic ways are utilized to identify those individuals desiring more knowledge about a personal relationship with Jesus Christ. First, through a *media campaign,* interested individuals are attracted by the life-changing testimonies on television and other media, and are given an opportunity to respond for a free booklet on how they can find new life in Christ. Second, through *systematic neighborhood campaigns,* in which each trained worker is assigned 50 telephone households, the telephone is used to identify interested individuals in a given neighborhood who want to know how to be closer to God.

From these two sources of names, the trained workers then make personal visits to share their Christian faith. These workers present the Christian message in such a way that it provides workable answers for the concerns which are uppermost in people's minds. In addition, they clearly show an individual how to receive Christ into his or her life. The Four Spiritual Laws, as illustrated in Exhibit 20.3, is used as the basic tool for communicating this Christian message. Other materials which amplify and expand upon this presentation are also utilized.

Initial Results

In 1975, the Here's Life, America movement began in the test city of Atlanta. During the spring of 1976, nineteen other metropolitan areas in the United States and Canada conducted Here's Life campaigns. As a result of these campaigns, 87,210 people have indicated they have trusted in Christ. More than 25,000 of these people have participated in follow-up Bible studies conducted by the more than 2,000 participating churches. As a further result of the movement, more than 52,000 Christians have been trained in evangelism and discipleship.

According to present plans, approximately 200 additional cities will present their media campaigns by the end of 1976. In addition, similar Here's Life movements are already underway or being planned for several other countries.

EXHIBIT 20.1
"I Found It!" Campaign Overview

"I FOUND IT!" CAMPAIGN OVERVIEW

Time		
6 to 2 weeks before Campaign	"Here's Life" Training Institute	Workers sign up, receive Campaign Worker Kits and complete Introductory Training Course. — Intro. Course Manual, Worker Kit, Worker Commitment Card
One week before Campaign	Your City	"Teaser Media Campaign" — I Found It! Billboards, T.V., Radio
Saturday before Campaign	Participating Church	**PRAYER RALLY** Workers are assigned to a Neighborhood Telephone Center (location & evening) and receive their Neighborhood Assignment Sheets. — Neighborhood Assignment Sheets
During 3 week Campaign	"I Found It" Telephone Center	Individuals respond to Media Campaign and request the "Here's How You Can Find It!" booklet. T.V., Billboards, I Found It!, Newspapers. Names are distributed to Neighborhood Telephone Centers.
Each week of Campaign	Neighborhood Telephone Center	Workers call *Media Responses* and set up personal appointments... Personal Appointment Cards ...to deliver "Here's How You Can Find It" booklet. Workers conduct "I Found It" telephone surveys from Neighborhood Assignment Sheets and set up personal appointments... ...to deliver "Beginning Your New Life" booklet.
Each week of Campaign	Neighborhoods	Workers make personal visits... to share booklets... and enroll interested individuals for Bible Study Classes to be held in each participating church
Last Saturday of Campaign	Participating Churches	**Praise Rally**—Workers share together what God has accomplished!
First Sunday after Campaign	Participating Churches	Follow-up **Bible Study Classes** begin and continue for 5 weeks.
After Campaign	Participating Churches involved in the Way of Life Plan	Weekly discipleship training classes are held with ongoing Neighborhood Way of Life Evangelism Teams.

HLA-025 Copyright 1976 Campus Crusade for Christ

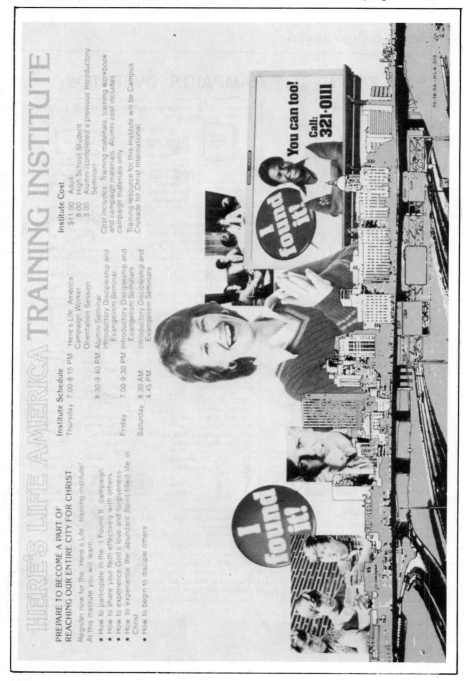

HERE'S LIFE AMERICA TRAINING INSTITUTE

**PREPARE TO BECOME A PART OF
REACHING OUR ENTIRE CITY FOR CHRIST**

Register now for the "Here's Life" training institute!
At this institute you will learn:

★ How to participate in the "I Found It" campaign
★ How to share your faith effectively with others
★ How to experience God's love and forgiveness
★ How to experience the abundant Spirit-filled life in Christ
★ How to begin to disciple others

Institute Schedule

Thursday 7:00-8:15 PM Here's Life America
Campaign Worker
Orientation Session

8:30-9:40 PM Alumni Seminar
Introductory Discipleship and
Evangelism Seminar

Friday 7:00-9:30 PM Introductory Discipleship and
Evangelism Seminars

Saturday 8:30 AM Introductory Discipleship and
4:45 PM Evangelism Seminars

Institute Cost

$11.00 Adult
8.00 High School Student
3.00 Alumni (completed a previous introductory Seminar)

Cost includes: Training materials, training workbook and campaign materials. Alumni cost includes campaign materials only.

Training resource for this institute will be Campus Crusade for Christ International.

I found it!
You can too!
Call: 321-0111

EXHIBIT 20.3
The Four Spiritual Laws

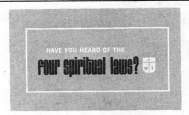

HAVE YOU HEARD OF THE

four spiritual laws?

Just as there are physical laws that govern the physical universe, so are there spiritual laws which govern your relationship with God.

LAW ONE

GOD **LOVES** YOU, AND HAS A WONDERFUL **PLAN** FOR YOUR LIFE.

(References contained in this booklet should be read in context from the Bible wherever possible.)

GOD'S LOVE

"For God so loved the world, that He gave His only begotten Son, that whoever believes in Him should not perish, but have eternal life" (John 3:16).

GOD'S PLAN

(Christ speaking) "I came that they might have life, and might have it abundantly" (that it might be full and meaningful) (John 10:10).

Why is it that most people are not experiencing the abundant life?

Because

LAW TWO

MAN IS **SINFUL** AND **SEPARATED** FROM GOD, THUS HE CANNOT KNOW AND EXPERIENCE GOD'S LOVE AND PLAN FOR HIS LIFE.

MAN IS SINFUL

"For all have sinned and fall short of the glory of God" (Romans 3:23).

Man was created to have fellowship with God; but, because of his own stubborn self-will, he chose to go his own independent way and fellowship with God was broken. This self-will, characterized by an attitude of active rebellion or passive indifference, is an evidence of what the Bible calls sin.

MAN IS SEPARATED

"For the wages of sin is death" (spiritual separation from God) (Romans 6:23).

God is holy and man is sinful. A great chasm separates the two. Man is continually trying to reach God and the abundant life through his own efforts: good life, ethics, philosophy, etc.

The Third Law gives us the only answer to this dilemma . . .

LAW THREE

JESUS CHRIST IS GOD'S **ONLY** PROVISION FOR MAN'S SIN. THROUGH HIM YOU CAN KNOW AND EXPERIENCE GOD'S LOVE AND PLAN FOR YOUR LIFE.

HE DIED IN OUR PLACE

"But God demonstrates His own love toward us, in that while we were yet sinners, Christ died for us" (Romans 5:8).

HE ROSE FROM THE DEAD

"Christ died for our sins . . . He was buried . . . He was raised on the third day according to the Scriptures . . . He appeared to Cephas, then to the twelve. After that He appeared to more than five hundred . . ." (I Corinthians 15:3-6).

HE IS THE ONLY WAY

"Jesus said to him, 'I am the way, and the truth, and the life; no one comes to the Father, but through Me'" (John 14:6).

God has bridged the chasm which separates us from Him by sending His Son, Jesus Christ, to die on the cross in our place.

It is not enough just to know these three laws . . .

LAW FOUR

WE MUST INDIVIDUALLY **RECEIVE** JESUS CHRIST AS SAVIOR AND LORD; THEN WE CAN KNOW AND EXPERIENCE GOD'S LOVE AND PLAN FOR OUR LIVES.

WE MUST RECEIVE CHRIST

"But as many as received Him, to them He gave the right to become children of God, even to those who believe in His name" (John 1:12).

WE RECEIVE CHRIST THROUGH FAITH

"For by grace you have been saved through faith; and that not of yourselves, it is the gift of God; not as a result of works, that no one should boast" (Ephesians 2: 8,9).

WE RECEIVE CHRIST BY PERSONAL INVITATION

(Christ is speaking): "Behold, I stand at the door and knock; if any one hears My voice and opens the door, I will come in to him" (Revelation 3:20).

Receiving Christ involves turning to God from self, trusting Christ to come into our lives, to forgive our sins and to make us what He wants us to be. It is not enough to give intellectual assent to His claims or to have an emotional experience.

These two circles represent two kinds of lives:

SELF-CONTROLLED LIFE
E—Ego or finite self on the throne
†—Christ outside the life
•—Interests controlled by self, often resulting in discord and frustration

CHRIST-CONTROLLED LIFE
†—Christ on the throne of the life
E—Ego—self dethroned
•—Interests under control of infinite God, resulting in harmony with God's plan

Which circle represents your life?
Which circle would you like to have represent your life?
The following explains how you can receive Christ:

YOU CAN RECEIVE CHRIST RIGHT NOW THROUGH PRAYER

(Prayer is talking with God)

God knows your heart and is not so concerned with your words as He is with the attitude of your heart. The following is a suggested prayer:

"Lord Jesus, I need You. I open the door of my life and receive You as my Savior and Lord. Thank You for forgiving my sins. Take control of the throne of my life. Make me the kind of person You want me to be."

Does this prayer express the desire of your heart?

If it does, pray this prayer right now, and Christ will come into your life, as He promised.

HOW TO KNOW THAT CHRIST IS IN YOUR LIFE

Did you receive Christ into your life? According to His promise in Revelation 3:20, where is Christ right now in relation to you? Christ said that He would come into your life. Would He mislead you? On what authority do you know that God has answered your prayer? (The trustworthiness of God Himself and His Word.)

THE BIBLE PROMISES ETERNAL LIFE TO ALL WHO RECEIVE CHRIST

"And the witness is this, that God has given us eternal life, and this life is in His Son. He who has the Son has the life; he who does not have the Son of God does not have the life. These things I have written to you who believe in the name of the Son of God, in order that you may know that you have eternal life" (I John 5:11-13).

Thank God often that Christ is in your life and that He will never leave you (Hebrews 13:5). You can know that the living Christ indwells you, and that you have eternal life, from the very moment you invite Him in on the basis of His promise. He will not deceive you. What about feelings?

CASE 21

U.S. POSTAL SERVICE

HOUSEHOLD CORRESPONDENCE ADVERTISING PROGRAM

The U.S. Postal Service (USPS), a quasi-independent corporation that replaced the old Post Office Department in 1971, has had financial difficulties ever since it was created. Latest budget estimates show the service expects continued heavy losses which could force officials to seek further rate boosts, decrease mail services, or request additional federal subsidies. The last rate increase took effect December 31, 1975 and included a 3 cent rise in first-class postage, to 13 cents for the first ounce.

Despite these higher rates, the Postal Service projects it will show a loss of $1.5 billion for the fiscal year ending June 30, 1976. These losses are strongly related to inflation increasing the service's operating costs at the same time that recession and rate increases have reduced mail volume for the first time since the Depression. The Postal Service, alarmed by the drop in mail use, is considering a nationwide advertising campaign urging people to write more letters.

Household Correspondence Marketing Program

The decline in mail usage began first and has hit hardest in the sector known as Household Correspondence, a relatively profitable area of first-class personal mail. In 1972, the average household was sending 3.8 pieces of personal mail per week. By 1974, the volume had dropped to 3.2, a decline of almost 16 percent in two years. A survey in the fall of 1975 indicated weekly volume was down even more to 2.6 pieces per average household.

In January 1975, the USPS began test marketing a business plan designed to build Household Correspondence letter-mail volume. The advertising program was developed to increase mail volume, which would result in improved productivity and higher revenues, with both factors helping to take some of the inflationary pressures off postal rates. Advertising in television, radio, magazines, and point-of-purchase ran in Columbus, Ohio, Minneapolis-St. Paul, and Atlanta. The business objective was to build a 10 percent increase in Household Correspondence which would yield approximately $100 million in annual incremental revenue on a national basis.

Advertising Strategy

The purpose of the test marketing is to find out if habits relating to personal correspondence can be influenced through the use of advertising. Specifically, the overall strategy in attempting advertising is to build postal revenues in the personal communications market by convincing people that writing is the most meaningful way of maintaining relationships with family and friends. Basic support in the advertisements is that writing, because it is a tangible gift of one's self, is the most welcome and appreciated form of communication.

J.T. Ellington, a Senior Assistant Postmaster General, states that the advertisements deal with the "inherent appeal of communication." For example, one of the television commercials shows a grandmother delighted at receiving a letter. A storyboard for a typical type of television commercial is shown in Exhibit 21.1. An example of the print advertisements is given in Exhibit 21.2.

"There is a quality of the mail that cannot be duplicated by the telephone," Ellington also says. "I grant that the telephone is more immediate and has aspects that are more personal, but the mail has other characteristics that cannot be duplicated by the phone. For example, you can send clippings and photographs and souvenirs to someone else." He adds that "this has a social value as well as being in our economic interests."

The Decision

Approximately $2 million has been spent on test marketing the advertising program. Results indicate that the revenue generated in the test markets is sufficient to pay for the cost of advertising as well as substantially contributing to new, net revenues for the USPS. The basic decision is whether or not to expand the advertising program. National implementation would incur media expenditures of about $12.1 million.

EXHIBIT 21.1
Storyboard for Typical Type of Television Advertisement

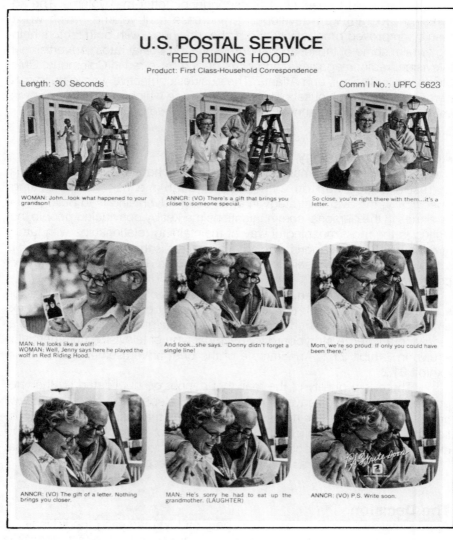

U.S. POSTAL SERVICE
"RED RIDING HOOD"
Product: First Class-Household Correspondence

Length: 30 Seconds   Comm'l No.: UPFC 5623

WOMAN: John...look what happened to your grandson!

ANNCR: (VO) There's a gift that brings you close to someone special.

So close, you're right there with them...it's a letter.

MAN: He looks like a wolf!
WOMAN: Well, Jenny says here he played the wolf in Red Riding Hood.

And look...she says. "Donny didn't forget a single line!

Mom, we're so proud. If only you could have been there."

ANNCR: (VO) The gift of a letter. Nothing brings you closer.

MAN: He's sorry he had to eat up the grandmother. (LAUGHTER)

ANNCR: (VO) P.S. Write soon.

EXHIBIT 21.2
Example of Print Advertisements

**Your letter is a gift
that brings you closer to all of them.**

One thing that makes a letter or card from you so special is that it can be shared by the people you love. And bring you closer to all of them.

That's because a letter is really a gift of yourself. It puts you right there with them, sharing what's on your mind. And in your heart.

The gift of a letter. There's nothing that brings you closer to someone special.

P.S. Write soon

© 1975, U.S. Postal Service

CASE 22

KEEP AMERICA BEAUTIFUL, INC.

CLEAN COMMUNITY SYSTEM

The basic purpose of Keep America Beautiful's Clean Community System is to control littering and to make municipalities cleaner, healthier, better places to live, by changing the attitudes and day-to-day trash handling habits of the entire community. It has achieved its purpose in test communities, which have sustained reduction in letter accumulation of up to 70 percent over a two-year period. But more importantly, it is fostering close cooperation between business and civic leaders and municipal officials to achieve mutually agreed upon goals. It is also creating a positive feeling on the part of citizens that they are not excluded from the decision-making process and that they have a positive role to play in the life and well-being of their municipality.

Background Information

Keep America Beautiful, Inc. was founded in 1953 by a group of forward-looking businessmen, largely from the beverage and packaging industry, as a national nonprofit public service organization to prevent littering. Since that time, KAB has led the way in a national movement to control litter and improve the environment, cooperating with government, industry, civic and service organizations in all 50 states. Today, 105 companies, trade associations, and labor unions, representing all sectors of the economy, support the organization. A National Advisory Council of 80 public service and professional organizations and 18 agencies of federal government guide KAB programming. Over 30 state and thousands of local affiliates carry out that program at the grass-roots level.

By 1972, however, it was evident that a more sophisticated approach was needed to deal with the growing litter problem brought about by increases in population, leisure time, and mobility. Early that year, KAB proposed to document empirically the impact of a comprehensive, community-owned and operated program to modify the physical, attitudinal, and situational factors contributing to litter.

With the help of a behavioral science consulting firm, KAB developed the Clean Community System as a program to control littering. The program was successfully field tested in three communities during 1974–1975. As of September 1976, the program was being implemented in 30 cities across America.

The CCS Program

Past experience has shown that unless local cleanups are part of a continuous, orderly, public education program, litter will return within days. KAB wants the Clean Community System program to be a "normative systems change process." That is, they desire to attract and keep people involved in coping with litter by helping them understand the psychological principles associated with littering and then getting them to change those norms that made littering acceptable.

Preliminary research identified five major sources of litter in addition to the two that usually come to mind, motorists and pedestrians. Improper household putouts, improper commercial putouts, carelessly maintained loading docks, construction and demolition sites, and uncovered trucks, KAB found, contributed more than half the trapped litter in most communities.

Descriptively, the preliminary research identified four groups of people whose norms relating to litter dynamics are critical to change. In motorists and pedestrians, these norms can be expressed as:

- ☐ "It's OK to litter where litter already is."
- ☐ "It's OK to litter where someone else is responsible for cleaning up."

☐ "It's OK to litter in places where the individual has no sense of ownership for the area."

The second group, the "gatekeepers," are those members of the community, such as municipal officials, property owners, and business managers, who make the decisions involving the containerization and removal of trash at their own operations and on public property. These individuals usually hold norms contributing to the littering problem that can be expressed as:

☐ "I've always run my operation this way."
☐ "It's somebody else's responsibility."
☐ "I'm only one, what I do won't make any difference."

Litter "witnesses" are those people who are irritated by litter, but whose norms are not to become involved, to avoid confrontation with the litterer or the "gatekeeper" who is contributing to the problem. The litter "victim" includes almost everyone who shares a sense of powerlessness about the problem and whose norms might be stated as:

☐ "Nobody else gives a damn, why should I?"
☐ "Those people (ghetto residents, sanitation workers, container manufacturers, fast food operators, or other scapegoats) are responsible for this mess."
☐ "You can't fight city hall."

Taken together, these attitudes make up the normative system which encourages littering. This is the network of norms, each reinforcing the other, that KAB's Clean Community System is designed to change. The program employs four components in attempting to change attitudes:

1. Adequate ordinances—assigning responsibility to both the public and private sectors for the containerization of trash and for the removal of trapped refuse.
2. Improved technology—the best equipment and practices to do the job within allocated resources, making better waste handling norms convenient and economical.
3. Continuous education—to make everyone aware of why and how their personal behavior contributes to the problem; to make new habits accepted, expected and the new "norm."
4. Effective enforcement—to persuade the recalcitrant few that the old, careless norms for waste handling will no longer be tolerated.

Implementation Plan

The key to the success of the program to date has been the "community involvement and ownership" of the program. The program can be sponsored by the local government agency, by business groups, or by civic organizations.

To make sure that communities gain the greatest benefit from their participation in the CCS program and its behavioral science techniques, KAB has set up a certification procedure. It requires the demonstrated support of local government, business, and the citizen force for adoption of the program, assurance that the community will commit the necessary funds ($3,000 to $5,000 for the first year, excluding the executive coordinator's salary and goods and services donated), and an agreement to send a three-person project team (one representative each from government, industry, and the voluntary sector) to a two-day training session conducted for KAB by the National Training and Development Service. In addition to factual content about the program, training sessions cover community organizing methods, group dynamics techniques, and the use of analysis and program materials prepared by KAB.

The community must also agree to purchase (at cost) the case of CCS program materials which include an organizing manual for the project team leader, litter/solid waste analysis guides, attitude survey forms and interviewing directions, a slide presentation on the normative systems approach to litter reduction, and manuals for subcommittee use. In return, KAB offers program and field counseling services and communications and information exchanges between participating communities.

Individual communities implement the CCS program through a five-step process:

1. Getting the facts—training workshops designed to clean up the confusion about litter, its sources, and its dynamics and to describe the norms that tend to encourage littering.
2. Involving the people—citizen's committee (representing all segments of local society) organized as an adjunct to city government, to develop a specific plan of action based on the facts identified through the training workshops and basic analysis and to be held accountable for fulfilling the plan.
3. Developing a systematic approach—integrating the four components (adequate ordinance, improved technology, continuous education, and effective enforcement) into an effective systematic approach to the litter problem.
4. Focusing on results—measuring litter accumulation before and after the program is implemented as a measure of its effectiveness.
5. Providing positive reinforcement—sustaining the new "norms" by rewarding improved trash handling habits through publicity, awards programs, and constant emphasis on the positive values of a cleaner environment.

In addition to the 30 cities currently implementing the Clean Community System, an additional 50 are processing applications for certification (as of September 1976) and well over 100 have expressed active interest in participation. Exhibit 22.1 indicates some of the results of the program for selected communities.

David A. Burkhalter, city manager of Charlotte, North Carolina, is representative of those directly involved in the program with this endorsement, "The Clean Community System is a workable, realistic approach to the litter problem. The program itself is best described as persuasive rather than mandatory, and, as a public administrator, I believe this approach is preferable in good government. Keep America Beautiful has developed a treatment for the litter problem, not simply small pieces of it. I wholeheartedly support it."

EXHIBIT 22.1
Measurements of Litter Accumulation in Certified System Communities

COMMUNITY	PERCENTAGE CHANGE a	MEASUREMENT TAKEN	BASE LINE TAKEN
Charlotte, N.C.	-72.2	June 1976	Feb. 1974
Evansville, Ind.	-40.3	May 1976	July 1975
Macon-Bibb County, Ga.	-57.0	Feb. 1976	April 1974
Monmouth, Ill.	-27.0	May 1976	April 1976
Reno/Sparks, Nev.	-33.6	March 1976	April 1975
Sioux Falls, S.D.	-50.9	May–June 1976	Sept. 1974
Tampa, Fla.	-78.0	May 1976	Feb. 1974

a Minus figures indicate reductions in litter accumulation.

PART EIGHT
COMPREHENSIVE CASES

CASE 23

WENDY'S INTERNATIONAL, INC. (B)
WENDY'S OLD FASHIONED HAMBURGERS

Wendy's International's only business is operating and franchising a hamburger chain called Wendy's Old Fashioned Hamburgers. While the firm is still a relatively young company, founded in 1969, it is well on its way to becoming an important factor in the franchise food industry[1]

Wendy's basic philosophy is to direct its product, place, and promotion toward the adult market, and through the adult, reach the family business. In terms of overall market positioning, the firm seems to be a step above the fast food hamburger operations like McDonald's, Burger King, and Burger Chef, while being a step below the inexpensive steak outlets like Bonanza and Ponderosa.

As of December 31, 1975, Wendy's had a total of 252 restaurants in operation. Of these, 69 were company owned and 183 were franchised. Management's goal is to have 1,000 units in operation by 1978. The target mix is to have 60 percent of these units franchised with the remainder being company owned.

[1]Study of this case should include a careful review of Wendy's International, Inc. (A).

Financial Performance

As shown in Exhibit 23.1, Wendy's has experienced substantial growth in revenues, expenses, and net income during the five-year period ending December 31, 1975. Operation of additional company-owned restaurants was the most significant factor in increased revenue and expense. However, as indicated by the average annual revenues of company-owned restaurants open 12 months or more, growth is also attributable to increases in volume per restaurant. Each franchise pays an amount equal to 4 percent of gross sales to the company as a franchise royalty. Prior to 1974, such payments constituted 2 percent or less of revenues. Royalty income was 4 percent of gross revenues in 1974 and 7 percent in 1975. Management expects royalties to continue to increase as a percentage of total revenues.

To gain a better understanding of the relative costs associated with running a Wendy's restaurant, Exhibit 23.2 presents a pro forma statement of annual operating expenses for two levels of gross sales. These figures would vary by certain localized factors and are not meant to represent any particular operating unit. They are used here for illustrative purposes only.

Marketing and Advertising Objectives

Wendy's basic marketing objective is to dominate local markets and to educate the consumer on Wendy's advantages over its competition. The firm identifies its target market as men and women between 18 and 49 years of age. Wendy's attempts to achieve its marketing objective by actively pursuing the following four points:

1. To introduce and promote the Wendy's Old Fashioned concept in the new market.
2. To provide a sales building plan for each market, whether franchise or home office.
3. To provide each market with the necessary materials and counsel.
4. To promote the pick-up window until it reaches a satisfactory percentage of volume.

Wendy's basic advertising objective is to consistently attract and retain new customers and to form favorable attitudes and opinions toward Wendy's Old Fashioned Hamburgers. Put more basically, the firm wants the consumer to feel that Wendy's products are better than those of the competition. Wendy's attempts to achieve its advertising objectives by actively pursuing the following five points:

1. To sell Wendy's theme of quality, choice, and freshness. To create positive attitudes toward the Wendy's concept.

2. To sell the pick-up window as highly convenient for "hurry" situations.
3. To sell the unlimited choice of condiments.
4. To sell the size of the hamburger.
5. To sell Wendy's features of rich, meaty chili, and thick Frosty.

Promotional Strategy

Wendy's promotional strategy is made up of extensive use of advertising, sales promotion (usually couponing), and publicity/public relations. Advertising media utilized include television, newspapers, radio, billboards, buscards, and taxitops, Each Wendy's restaurant spends about 4 percent of sales on advertising. Exhibits 23.3, 23.4, and 23.5 represent typical examples of advertisements used in newspaper, television, and radio, respectively.

Coupons are used by Wendy's as a promotional device to increase sales movement or heighten awareness on a short-term basis which will hopefully retain some residual benefit for return customers. They provide an opportunity for the consumer to save money and are also used on occasions as an encouragement to try new products. Coupons used by Wendy's generally offer a free item with the purchase of another one or two menu items at regular price, or a discount off a regular price item. Based on test situations Wendy's has found that the most frequently redeemed coupons have been those distributed through newspaper advertisements and direct mail because of the greater selectivity of saturation per dollar spent.

Wendy's also focuses on cultivating a good relationship with the public in the market it operates in. Local restaurants are encouraged to take part in public activities and community programs. Examples of such participation include joining in local parades, sponsoring a queen in a pageantry, and making tickets available for local sporting and cultural events.

Marketing Research

In order to learn more about the relative importance of various restaurant characteristics and how Wendy's compares with other hamburger restaurants on those characteristics, a marketing research project was undertaken in one of Wendy's primary markets. Potential respondents were randomly selected from the local telephone directory and then called to solicit cooperation in the study. If a respondent agreed to participate a questionnaire was mailed for his or her completion. Wendy's was not identified as the primary restaurant under study.

In addition to the standard demographic variables such as age, income, occupation, sex, education, etc., respondents were asked the following questions:

> How *important* is it to you that a fast food restaurant satisfy you on the following characteristics? Circle "1" if the characteristic is very important or "6" if the characteristic is very unimportant, or somewhere in between depending on how important it is to you that the restaurant satisfy you on the characteristic. (Eleven characteristics were presented to the respondent, each with a six-point scale to measure the level of importance.)

> Please indicate how much you think each of the fast food restaurants *has* of the following characteristics. Circle a "1" if you think the restaurant is high in the characteristic, a "6" if you think it is low in the characteristic, or somewhere in between depending on how much of the characteristic you think the restaurant has. Please give your opinion of every restaurant on each characteristic even if you have to guess. (Seven characteristics were presented to the respondent, along with a six-point scale to measure Burger Chef, Burger King, McDonald's, and Wendy's on each of the characteristics.)

> Following are a series of questions regarding your attitudes toward fast food restaurants. To each question please indicate whether you STRONGLY AGREE, AGREE, DON'T KNOW (NEUTRAL), DISAGREE, or STRONGLY DISAGREE. There are no right or wrong answers: We only want to know what YOU think. (Respondents were then presented with a series of specific statements, along with a five-point scale to indicate their degree of agreement with each statement.)

> How important do you consider each of the following as sources of information about fast food restaurants? Check one for each item listed. (Respondents were then presented with seven information sources and asked to indicate if each was important, somewhat important, or not important.)

A total of 775 respondents returned questionnaires which were usable for most of the analysis. The actual number of respondents varied for each question due to errors of completion and errors of omission. Results for each question are presented in Exhibit 23.6 in terms of percentages of respondents giving each of the possible answers.

EXHIBIT 23.1
Historical Financial Summary
of Wendy's International, Inc.
Five-Year Period 1971–1975
(Years Ended December 31)

	1971	1972	1973	1974	1975
Revenues	$ 683,967	$1,834,118	$4,540,931	$12,600,524	$29,583,705
Cost of sales	391,894	979,602	2,372,883	6,402,173	14,674,624
Operating expenses	226,357	649,184	1,449,157	3,675,616	8,939,251
Interest expense	9,878	23,134	135,434	338,203	805,570
Income before taxes	55,838	182,198	583,457	2,134,532	5,164,260
Net income	45,570	108,498	327,257	1,129,058	2,747,260
Earnings per share	.02	.05	.11	.36	.84
Total assets	397,165	1,728,700	4,735,835	11,713,249	21,747,079
Shareholders' equity	151,417	949,534	1,572,159	3,037,288	6,809,645
Number of shares outstanding	2,250,000	2,775,000	3,011,610	3,061,610	3,155,715
Pretax margin	8.16%	9.93%	12.84%	16.94%	17.46%
Return on equity [a]	54.48%	19.70%	25.95%	48.99%	55.80%
Sales—Company owned & franchised	681,804	2,014,567	6,263,848	24,232,962	74,462,639
Number of restaurants in operation					
Company owned	4	9	32	93	252
Franchised	4	7	17	42	69
	—	2	15	51	183
Average annual revenues of company owned restaurants open 12 months or longer	265,644	345,165	390,012	438,879	463,419

[a] Based on average equity employed.

EXHIBIT 23.2
Pro Forma Statement of Operations for a Wendy's Outlet
(Through December 31, 1975) Two Levels of Annual Gross Sales

SALES	$300,000	100.00%	$500,000	100.00%
Cost of goods sold				
Manager or owner	$ 13,000	4.33%	$ 13,000	2.60%
Co-manager	10,500	3.50	10,500	2.10
Crew	27,750	9.25	42,500	8.50
Total labor	$ 51,250	17.08%	$ 66,000	13.20%
Food	111,000	37.00	185,000	37.00
Paper	12,000	4.00	20,000	4.00
Laundry	1,050	.35	1,750	.35
Total cost of goods sold	$175,300	58.43%	$272,750	54.55%
Gross profit	$124,700	41.57%	$227,250	45.45%
Operating Expenses				
Rent	$ 25,800	8.60%	$ 25,800	5.16%
Royalty	12,000	4.00	20,000	4.00
Insurance	2,100	.70	2,100	.42
Taxes—payroll	3,450	1.15	5,000	1.00
Taxes—real estate	2,000	.67	2,000	.40
Taxes—other	1,000	.33	1,000	.20
Supplies	3,750	1.25	6,250	1.25
Utilities	10,250	3.42	11,250	2.25
Repair & maintenance	4,500	1.50	5,000	1.00
Telephone	500	.17	500	.10
Trash removal	1,500	.50	1,500	.30
Advertising & promotion	12,000	4.00	20,000	4.00
Office expenses	1,200	.40	1,200	.24
Micellaneous	250	.08	250	.05
Total operating expenses	$ 80,300	26.77%	$101,850	20.37%
Cash flow	$ 44,400	14.80%	$125,400	25.08%
Depreciation	6,000	2.00	6,000	1.20
Pretax profit	$ 38,400	12.80%	$119,400	23.88%

EXHIBIT 23.3
Example of Print Advertisement for Wendy's

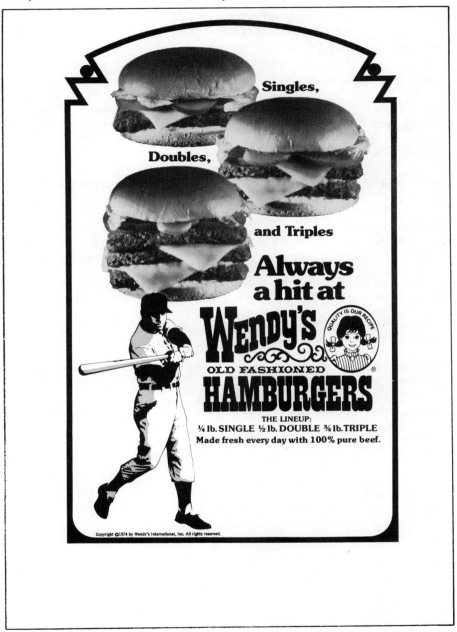

EXHIBIT 23.4
Example of Continuity of Television Commercial for Wendy's

WENDY'S INTERNATIONAL, INC.
(FROSTY) "A COOL, FRESH FINISH"

VIDEO	AUDIO	
Open on MCU Gals at Wendy's Counter	1st GIRL:	Two great-tasting Wendy's Old Fashioned Hamburgers
	2nd GIRL:	. . . and two french fries.
MCU Mgr. Zoom into CU	MANAGER:	Followed by a cool cup of our exclusive Frosty.
Cut to MCU Gals at Counter	1st GIRL:	Alright!
	2nd GIRL:	Me, too!
Dissolve to Wendy Gal at Frosty Machine	WENDY GAL:	Two cool, creamy Frostys coming up.
Dissolve to MCU Guy at Counter	MAN:	A bowl of chili and a—uh—
Cut to MCU Manager	MANAGER:	Frosty.
Cut to MCU Man	MAN:	Yeah—a Frosty.
Cut to CU Wendy Gal	WENDY GAL:	Frosty our fresh all-natural dairy dessert.
Dissolve to Tray Shot of Frosty, Chili, French Fries, Hamburger	MGR. V.O.:	It's a cool, fresh finish to your Wendy's favorites.
LS of Dining Area Zoom in Past Gals Table to Guy Eating Frosty	2nd GIRL:	It's so thick you have to eat it with a spoon.
Dissolve to Image Store Top Half of Screen with Super: "Fresh Tastes Best"	VOCAL UP:	*At Wendy's Old Fashioned Hamburgers Fresh Tastes Best.*
	Instrumental Reprise Out	

EXHIBIT 23.5
Example of Continuity of Radio Commercial for Wendy's

60 SECOND ANNOUNCEMENT
WENDY'S INTERNATIONAL, INC.

SFX: Low Key Outdoor Sounds—Pedestrian and Vehicular Traffic

NARRATOR:	1	Hello. Join me in a visit to a different kind
	2	of convenience restaurant—a restaurant that
	3	in many ways is a lot like bygone days. It's
	4	called Wendy's—Wendy's Old Fashioned Hamburgers.
	5	*Replace Outdoor SFX with Indoor Muted Crowd Sounds*
	6	Look around. Notice the carpeting, the Victorian parlor
	7	beads, the Tiffany lamps, and bentwood chairs. But best
	8	of all—everything that Wendy's prepares is fresh.
	9	Because fresh tastes best.
GIRL:	10	Hi. Welcome to Wendy's Old Fashioned Hamburgers.
	11	May I take your order?
NARRATOR:	12	Yes . . . but is it true you have a creed at Wendy's to
	13	make sure everything is fresh?
GIRL:	14	It's true. Our hamburgers are 100 percent pure
	15	beef, never frozen, and pattied fresh daily.
	16	We cook each sandwich to order with what you want
	17	on it, never pre-wrapped.
	18	Because quality is our recipe.
NARRATOR:	19	"Quality is our recipe." That says a lot.
GIRL:	20	It's what our creed is all about. We start fresh
	21	every day because we know that fresh tastes best.
VOCAL UP	22	*At Wendy's*
	23	*Fresh Tastes Best*
	24	*Instrumental Reprise 6-Sec. under Live Store Addresses*
	25	

EXHIBIT 23.6
Results of Consumer Research on Selected Fast Food Restaurants

Importance of characteristics in the selection of fast food restaurants.

	Very Important 1	2	3	4	5	Very Unimportant 6	Average Score
Speed of service	47.1%	22.1%	13.8%	7.8%	5.0%	4.2%	2.14
Variety of menu	26.7	20.1	22.3	14.5	9.5	6.9	2.81
Popularity with children	22.9	13.1	11.6	9.9	10.4	32.1	3.68
Cleanliness	77.6	8.7	2.9	1.9	1.9	6.9	1.63
Convenience	61.0	18.2	8.5	4.0	3.2	5.0	1.85
Taste of food	75.9	12.4	3.4	1.4	1.5	5.3	1.56
Price	44.6	19.1	13.5	8.2	7.2	7.5	2.37
Drive-in window	10.7	9.6	13.2	11.5	13.9	41.1	4.32
Friendliness of personnel	44.2	20.6	17.2	6.8	5.1	6.2	2.27
Quality of french fries	46.4	21.2	11.1	8.8	4.6	7.9	2.28
Taste of hamburgers	65.7	14.4	5.2	4.9	2.4	7.4	1.86

Ratings of selected restaurants on specific characteristics.

	Food Tastes Very Good 1	2	3	4	5	Food Tastes Very Bad 6	Average Score
Burger Chef	9.8%	13.8%	22.0%	19.9%	19.9%	14.6%	3.70
Burger King	12.0	17.3	25.6	24.3	14.6	6.2	3.31
McDonald's	32.4	26.0	21.9	11.6	4.6	3.5	2.40
Wendy's	35.7	20.1	17.9	12.6	8.5	5.2	2.54

	Extremely Clean 1	2	3	4	5	Extremely Unclean 6	Average Score
Burger Chef	10.9%	23.2%	23.5%	18.2%	15.6%	8.7%	3.30
Burger King	15.3	24.4	27.7	18.4	10.0	4.3	2.96
McDonald's	40.9	27.8	18.7	6.2	3.5	2.9	2.12
Wendy's	32.9	29.2	16.0	12.2	5.3	4.3	2.41

	Close to Where I Am 1	2	3	4	5	Out of the Way 6	Average Score
Burger Chef	34.1%	15.1%	16.3%	11.7%	8.7%	14.1%	2.88
Burger King	22.4	13.5	12.9	16.9	13.9	19.4	3.45
McDonald's	47.5	19.3	10.8	7.3	6.0	9.1	2.32
Wendy's	35.6	17.8	16.5	10.0	9.0	11.3	2.73

	Low Cost Menu 1	2	3	4	5	6	Average Score
Burger Chef	28.8%	32.6%	24.8%	9.0%	3.5%	1.3%	2.30
Burger King	17.7	27.7	32.9	15.2	5.1	1.4	2.66
McDonald's	46.4	25.4	20.3	5.6	1.4	.9	1.93
Wendy's	11.1	18.3	24.7	19.5	14.8	11.6	3.43

EXHIBIT 23.6 *(Continued)*

	Very Fast Service						Average Score
	1	2	3	4	5	6	
Burger Chef	21.1%	27.4%	25.3%	12.7%	8.3%	5.2%	2.75
Burger King	26.5	27.9	25.0	13.4	5.7	1.5	2.49
McDonald's	61.7	20.1	9.1	4.1	2.1	2.3	1.71
Wendy's	42.5	25.7	15.3	9.4	5.1	2.0	2.15

	Children Like the Food Very Much				Children Don't Like the Food at All		Average Score
	1	2	3	4	5	6	
Burger Chef	30.7%	28.1%	20.7%	10.8%	5.9%	3.8%	2.44
Burger King	22.1	33.5	21.7	14.1	5.4	3.2	2.57
McDonald's	67.8	17.6	9.7	2.3	1.3	1.3	1.55
Wendy's	32.5	25.7	18.8	12.0	7.6	3.3	2.47

	Wide Variety Menu				Narrow Variety Menu		Average Score
	1	2	3	4	5	6	
Burger Chef	18.8%	16.4%	25.4%	19.5%	12.7%	7.3%	3.12
Burger King	18.2	15.9	26.4	21.5	12.2	5.8	3.11
McDonald's	31.4	16.2	23.3	14.6	9.2	5.3	2.70
Wendy's	21.8	20.1	21.1	16.4	12.3	8.3	3.02

Degree of agreement with selected statements about fast food dining.

	Strongly Agree 1	Agree 2	Don't Know 3	Disagree 4	Strongly Disagree 5	Average Score
I prefer fast food restaurants which have many different items on their menu	28.0%	37.1%	10.3%	21.7%	2.9%	2.35
Children in our household have a say where the family eats	18.9	40.2	19.4	14.0	7.5	2.51
The easiest way to judge a fast food hamburger restaurant is by the quality of the french fries	5.7	17.0	20.5	38.2	18.6	3.47
All fast food hamburgers taste the same	11.3	11.0	4.7	39.8	33.2	3.73
The way a fast food store is decorated is important to me	17.4	32.4	11.6	31.0	7.7	2.79
If a fast food restaurant has an atmosphere similar to that of a regular restaurant I feel more comfortable going to it	12.9	40.7	15.4	25.9	5.1	2.70
I am more interested in the taste of a hamburger, not if the meat were frozen or ground fresh daily	20.1	50.8	6.8	14.3	8.0	2.40
I would rather specify what topping I want on a hamburger than buy one that is precooked and prewrapped	44.0	33.0	8.7	12.5	1.9	1.95

EXHIBIT 23.6 (Continued)

I consider a hamburger made of frozen meat to taste better than one where the meat was fresh	8.4	3.8	37.5	33.2	17.2 3.47
I prefer fast food restaurants that have a drive-in window	3.2	14.4	22.7	42.9	16.8 3.56

Importance of sources of information about fast food restaurants.

	Important	Somewhat Important	Not Important
Television	44.0%	31.3%	24.8%
Radio	29.7	39.5	30.8
Newspapers	32.9	40.1	27.0
Magazines	8.8	36.8	54.4
Billboards	18.6	37.7	43.7
Friends or relatives	58.1	25.6	16.3
Mail	11.6	27.0	61.4

CASE 24

KALSØ SYSTEMET, INC.
THE EARTH® SHOE[1]

No brand of shoe in the history of the shoe industry has received the recognition and acclaim bestowed upon the Earth® brand shoe. The world's first negative heel shoe, with its unique patented sole, was invented by Anne Kalso in Copenhagen in 1957 and introduced in New York in 1970. The Earth shoe has become a fashion phenomenon with over 140 stores in the United States and Canada doing a booming business in the shoe and other Earth brand products.

How It All Began
Anne Kalsø, a Danish Yoga teacher, has always had an intense interest in the well-being of the mind and body based on her early attraction to ancient cultures and philosophies. In Santos, Brazil, in the course of her studies and experiments in Yoga, she observed that by flexing the foot or lowering the heel one could achieve a physical feeling similar to that attained in the lotus

---

[1]The Earth® shoe is a registered trademark for Kalso Systemet, Inc.

position. This awareness inspired her to develop, in 1957 (with the aid of a Portuguese shoemaker) a primitive version of a sandal with the heel lower than the toes.

For ten years she developed and refined her designs to the form that the Earth shoe takes today. In commenting on her personal tests of the models she states, "It took numerous years of hard work before I reached the final form of my shoe which takes into consideration all the natural demands of the foot and body. Now I know that I have created something. It is no longer an idea in my mind, but a thoroughly tested and proven fact." Basic attributes of the Earth shoe are described in Exhibit 24.1.

Raymond and Eleanor Jacobs were in Copenhagen in the summer of 1969 where Eleanor purchased a pair of Anne Kalsø's shoes. After wearing the shoes for two weeks and realizing how comfortable and remarkable they were, Eleanor and Raymond contacted Mrs. Kalsø about the possibilities of distributing the shoes in the United States. She agreed to talk with them after finding out he was a professional photographer and she an artist, rather than individuals in the shoe business. Mrs. Kalsø explained later that she had been approached by many shoe companies but rejected their proposals because they did not fully "understand" the significance of her product, what it meant to her, and what she had gone through to develop it.

On April 1, 1970, which coincidentally, was the first celebration of Earth Day in the United States and around the world, the Jacobs opened their first shoe store in New York. it was on that day that Anne Kalsø's shoe was named Earth.

Expanding Distribution

The first store was opened for about six months when customers, who believed in the shoes and were attracted to the way the Jacobs' did business, began making inquiries about how they could get involved in selling the Earth negative heel shoes. The first stores were opened by satisfied customers, mostly in university towns. Late in 1972, the company purchased a factory in New England and the first Earth brand shoes made in America started rolling off the production line.

There are now over 140 stores selling the Earth brand shoes with 10 being company owned and the rest in the hands of private owners. Many of the owners and store personnel have had no previous shoe-industry experience. No two stores are identical, although most interiors use wood and natural colors extensively and, in general, reflect a casual, comfortable "personality." A variety of plants, woven rugs, and bulletin boards for community news add to this image.

The Earth shoes often are displayed on pedestals, as in a sculpture gallery, and the furniture ranges from contemporary canvas chairs to antique wooden benches. The company has no requirements for the architecture of the individually owned stores, and even the company-owned stores vary in appearance. The stores sell only Earth brand shoes and Earth apparel, including woolen hats and scarves and patented wide-toe socks.

The company is now in the process of planning a major expansion. What started as a "cult" has become a major brand with the product being worn by all age groups in every community. The firm is not involved in a franchise type of operation. Instead the company is merely the seller of the shoes and the store owners are the buyers.

Store owners invest their money in start-up costs, fixtures, and inventory. At the present time, the capital required to open an Earth shoe store is estimated at from $30,000 to $100,000, depending on the market, location, site of the store, and the cost necessary for renovation or building construction. The company assists the individual owners with such advisory services as store opening materials, training programs, display materials, business form, etc. The company also conducts marketing research programs and national advertising campaigns.

Promotional Communications

Individual stores, company as well as private, do their own local advertising. However, the company provides advertising mats which are prepared at the company's expense. Store owners may or may not use them as they see fit. One example of a local retail advertising campaign is shown in Exhibit 24.2. This type of advertisement was used to announced "The First Sale on Earth." Most stores around the country participated in this three-week program and reported excellent sales.

The company sponsors national advertising campaigns using print media such as *Newsweek, Psychology Today, Rolling Stone, Time, Cosmopolitan, Glamour, Ms., National Lampoon, Seventeen,* and others. An example advertisement from one such campaign is show in Exhibit 24.3.

Using a toll-free number at the bottom of the advertisements represents an important change in the company's strategic approach to communications. At one point the firm listed the locations of stores in its print advertising. This new approach allows the interested person to contact a trained operator for additional information.

The procedure works as follows: A person calls the number free (Kalsø Systemet, Inc. pays for all calls in the United States) and reaches an operator who responds to questions and takes the callers' name, address, etc. If there is a store within 100 miles of the person's call, he or she is given the address of the Earth shoe store or stores. The store then receives a copy of the recorded call, with all the pertinent information filled in. In this way, the store can better serve the caller by either mailing a brochure or answering whatever questions have been asked.

In late 1975, the company started its first national advertising on national television. The advertisement was designed to tie in with certain national print campaigns. Initial advertising in this campaign appeared on "Cronkite News," "The Tomorrow Show," "The Tonight Show," "Midnite Special," and "Saturday Night."

Summary Observations

Eleanor Jacobs, in reviewing the firm's initial strategies, its present successes, and future directions, offers the following observations:

> Presently, the Earth brand shoe is sold only in Earth shoe stores. We made that decision when we brought the shoes to the United States back in 1969. Since we believed in the principle of this shoe, we felt it would be inconsistent for us to sell them alongside high-heeled platform shoes. We sell them because we believe in their unprecedented comfort and although we do not make any medical claims, our grateful customers send us loving testimonial letters attesting not only to their comfort, but attributing to them all kinds of benefits. Although many of us have experienced personal benefits from wearing the shoes (especially me!), we are careful not to emphasize that aspect of the shoe since no shoe is a panacea for all people.

> We are rather proud of Anne Kalsø as well as the philosophy and marketing approach which this company has taken because, if we have accomplished nothing else, we have managed to revolutionize the shoe industry's awareness of the importance of comfort when designing casual shoes. There are currently over 100 manufacturers imitating the look of our shoe, which is understandable. They are along for the fashion ride. However, the look-alikes do not function like the Earth brand shoe.

> We continue to research and improve the structure and design of the shoe and Anne Kalsø is deeply involved with us as a consultant and expert on the subject. She was 71 years old in January and lives most of the year in Toronto where she is continuing to develop programs and concepts which she hopes will provide city dwellers with the opportunity to counteract the unnatural (cement and asphalt) environmental conditions under which they must live.

EXHIBIT 24.1
Basic Attributes of the Earth Negative Heel Shoe

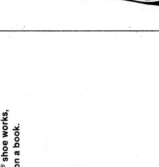

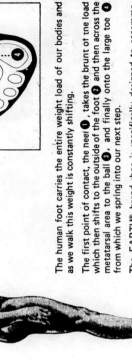

about the EARTH® negative heel shoe.

To get an idea of how the EARTH® shoe works, stand barefoot with your toes up on a book. Feel what begins to happen.

Wearing the EARTH® brand shoe, you will experience a completely new way of walking that might take some getting used to. Initially, you may feel off-balance because of the negative heel. This is normal so don't be alarmed. Young people adapt very quickly, older people take a little longer . . .

In effect, you are walking barefoot on the beach . . . or across summer fields . . . wherever you go. Because walking in EARTH® brand shoes is a form of exercise, some may at first experience stiffness in the calves or thighs; some may find our unique arch may take getting used to; so moderate wear is advised in the beginning.

The uniquely contoured sole will allow you to walk in a gentle rolling motion. This helps to develop a more natural, graceful walk. There is no reason why you cannot interchange the use of other shoes with the EARTH® brand shoe.

The human foot carries the entire weight load of our bodies and as we walk this weight is constantly shifting.

The first point of contact, the heel ❶, takes the brunt of the load which then shifts to the outside of the foot ❷ and then across the metatarsal area to the ball ❸, and finally onto the large toe ❹ from which we spring into our next step.

The EARTH® brand shoe is specifically designed to accommodate the shifting of weight load on our feet with the greatest ease and comfort.

Another feature of the EARTH® brand shoe is the unique arch support.

EXHIBIT 24.2
Example of Local Print Advertisement

EXHIBIT 24.3
Example of National Print Advertisement

CASE 25

DIVERSIFIED INFORMATION SYSTEMS CORPORATION

COMPUTER SOFTWARE AND HARDWARE-INSURANCE INDUSTRY

For several years Bob N. Daniel, a general agent and later vice-president of a major life insurance company used a rather unique program to further serve the insurance needs of his more sophisticated clients. This program enabled him to show many individuals how their current life insurance coverage could be increased 50 to 300 percent with little or no additional out-pocket cash outlay.

Convinced that other agents could also successfully use the program, Daniel decided to form a company to develop the necessary computer software compatible with existing mini-computers, and market the total computer and software package to insurance companies and individual insurance agencies. To that end, Diversified Information Systems Corporation (DISC) was organized in 1974.

The Basic Concept

Over the years most people have built up loan values in their whole life insurance policies. Provisions in most policies allow the owner of the policy to borrow against these values, usually at relatively low interest rates such as 5 or 6 percent. In addition, provided certain basic conditions are met, the Internal Revenue Service permits the interest payments on such loans to be treated as deductions for individuals who file itemized tax returns.

A basic objective of DISC's Computer Analyzed Programs (CAP) is to develop a personalized, time-phased program for an agent to show an individual how to more effectively manage a total life insurance program consistent with these specific objectives established for that program. The underlying idea is to confine a person's annual cash commitments for life insurance with present and future values of the policies, to maximize the total amount of insurance coverage with minimum out-of-pocket expense. A premise developed by Daniel and proven by the computer study illustrations is that "everyone would like to have more life insurance coverage, but no one wants to pay additional premiums." This premise is conveyed to the prospective purchaser by statements such as:

1. "Mr. Prospect, if you're paying for it (additional coverage that he has been 'paying' for but doesn't own) shouldn't you have it?"
2. "If I can add a substantial amount of life insurance coverage to your present estate without requiring additional cash outlay, would you take it?"

Based on:

1. the present loan values of existing policies
2. anticipated dividends and loan values building in all policies
3. the tax bracket of the policy owner
4. remaining years of payments of the policies

and other factors, CAP provides a prospective insurance client with a computer printout of easily digested, key planning figures. These figures include such items as

1. required annual cash commitments
2. annual tax savings
3. cash values
4. dividends
5. liquidating cash value
6. net death proceeds for each year for any specified number of years

Such a computer output (called a "Computer Study") enables the insurance agent to show a client the impact of alternative decisions on that person's total life insurance package. A sample computer output is shown in Exhibit 25.1. To add to an understanding of the system and its uses, Exhibit 25.2 lists some descriptive excerpts taken from promotional brochures.

The Product Offering

A "DISC System" consists of three main components:

1. *The software*—the DISC computer analyzed programs consist of some eighteen separate software capabilities including
   a. leverage proposal service
   b. simplified servicing programs
   c. capital needs analysis
   d. split dollar
2. *The hardware*—mini-computers manufactured by major manufacturers with 32K byte memory and 2½ million byte disk storage (alternative computer sizes and storage capacities available)
3. *Supporting equipment*—various terminals, desk for housing computer, cathode ray tubes, high speed printers, etc.

Training manuals for a DISC system and its implementation, and all required input and proposal forms are also furnished to each DISC system user. Installation of the system is handled by DISC trained personnel. Each purchaser is also invited to attend a schooling program designed to instruct insurance personnel in how to get the maximum benefit from the total system ("programs" noted above are not owned by the purchaser but the lifetime "license agreements" to the software package developed by DISC).

The standard system involving the above components is priced at $46,900.00. Systems with greater capacities are available. The firm also offers a wide variety of leasing in lieu of an outright purchase.

Marketing Efforts

During the first year of DISC's operation, a major portion of the marketing effort consisted of personal visits by Daniel and other associates to selected insurance companies and agencies. An Executive model motor home was equipped with a complete DISC computer system so that on-the-spot demonstrations could be performed. Additional prospective purchasers have made visits to DISC Corporate headquarters for personal demonstrations. The majority of these early contacts came from Daniel's personal acquaintances within the insurance industry and in turn from their personal recommendations to others.

In mid-1976, in an attempt to reach larger groups of potential purchasers, associates of DISC began to demonstrate the computer system at professional meetings of life insurance agents. One such meeting, the Million Dollar Round Table held in Boston, Massachusetts, generated over 100 requests for specific follow-up information.

While all of these approaches led to a reasonable level of sales volume, the DISC system was not reaching sales forecast. As stated by William O. Gardner, Vice-President of Marketing for DISC, there is a problem in developing "the ability to move the potential client from the point of an intense interest (which he or she immediately develops when shown the system) to the place of being willing to commit for as big a ticket item as the ticket is. Although most agents readily understand the tremendous potential that the DISC system would generate, yet nevertheless, it seems a too difficult leap for them to make this commitment which is probably the first or second largest financial commitment that many of them have ever made."

EXHIBIT 25.1
Sample Computer Output from DISC's Computer Analyzed Program (CAP)

YEAR	AGE	1. ANNUAL CASH COMMITMENT BEFORE TAX	2. ANNUAL TAX SAVINGS	3. ANNUAL COMMITMENT AFTER TAX	4. CUMULATIVE COMMITMENT BEFORE TAX	5. CUMULATIVE COMMITMENT AFTER TAX	6. INSURANCE CASH VALUES	7. CASH VALUE OF PAID UP ADDITIONS	8. INSURANCE LOANS	9. NET INS. SURRENDER VALUES 6+7-8	10. OTHER LOANS (Previous to this program)	11. DIVIDEND OR OTHER EQUITIES	12. LIQUIDATING CASH VALUE 9+11-10	13. INSURANCE FACE AMOUNT	14. NET DEATH PROCEEDS 13+11-8-10
1975	35	1874	0	1874	1874	1874	10840	0	1405	9435	0	0	9435	200000	198595
1976	36	1943	69	1874	3817	3748	14020	0	3381	10639	0	0	10639	200000	196619
1977	37	1943	69	1874	5760	5622	17300	0	5128	12172	0	0	12172	200000	194872
1978	38	2016	142	1874	7775	7496	20720	0	6934	13786	0	0	13786	200000	193066
1979	39	2015	141	1874	9790	9370	24140	0	8655	15484	0	0	15484	200000	191344
1980	40	2087	213	1874	11877	11244	27420	0	10427	16993	0	0	16993	200000	191573
1981	41	2086	212	1874	13963	13118	30700	0	12115	18585	0	0	18585	200000	190573
1982	42	2157	283	1874	16120	14992	33980	0	13851	20129	0	0	20129	200000	187885
1983	43	2190	316	1874	18310	16866	37380	0	15566	21814	0	0	21814	200000	186149
1984	44	2224	350	1874	20534	18740	40780	0	17270	23510	0	0	23510	200000	184434
1985	45	2258	384	1874	22792	20614	44300	0	18962	25338	0	0	25338	200000	182730
1986	46	2289	415	1874	25081	22488	47820	0	20576	27244	0	0	27244	200000	181038
1987	47	2320	446	1874	27401	24362	51340	0	22112	29228	0	0	29228	200000	179424
1988	48	2349	475	1874	29750	26236	54832	0	23572	31260	0	0	31260	200000	177888
1989	49	2376	502	1874	32126	28110	58324	0	24955	33368	0	0	33368	200000	176428
1990	50	2402	528	1874	34528	29984	61955	0	26258	35697	0	0	35697	200000	175045
1991	51	2426	552	1874	36954	31858	65587	0	27478	38109	0	0	38109	200000	173742
1992	52	2448	574	1874	39402	33732	69219	0	28611	40607	0	0	40607	200000	172522
1993	53	2469	595	1874	41871	35606	72851	0	29655	43195	0	0	43195	200000	171388
1994	54	2488	614	1874	44359	37480	76482	0	30606	45876	0	0	45876	200000	170345
1995	55	2505	630	1874	46864	39354	79924	0	31460	48464	0	0	48464	200000	169374
1996	56	2519	645	1874	49383	41228	83364	0	32206	51160	0	0	51160	200000	168794
1997	57	2532	658	1874	51913	43102	86808	0	32839	53968	0	0	53968	200000	167161
1998	58	2542	668	1874	54455	44976	90249	0	33356	56894	0	0	56894	200000	166444
1999	59	2550	676	1874	57005	46850	93691	0	33751	59940	0	0	59940	200000	166249
2000	60	2555	681	1874	59560	48724	97133	0	34021	63112	0	0	63112	200000	165779
2001	61	2558	684	1874	62117	50598	100575	0	34160	66415	0	0	66415	200000	165840
2002	62	2558	684	1874	64675	52472	104016	0	34164	69853	0	0	69853	200000	165836
2003	63	2558	684	1874	67233	54346	107458	0	34032	73427	0	0	73427	200000	165968
2004	64	2555	681	1874	69788	56220	110900	0	33759	77141	0	0	77141	200000	166241
2005	65	138		138	69925	56220	110900	0	27174	83726	0	0	83726	200000	172826

SUMMARY COMPARISON

TAX BRACKETS USED IN CALCULATIONS
START # THROUGH · EQUITY · START # · EQUITY
35% · 2005 · 0% · A · 450x · 0%

	YEAR 1975			YEAR 1984			YEAR 1994			YEAR 2005		
	PROPOSED	ORIGINAL	DIFFERENCE	PROPOSED	ORIGINAL	DIFFERENCE	PROPOSED	ORIGINAL	DIFFERENCE	PROPOSED	ORIGINAL	DIFFERENCE
OUTLAY BEFORE TAX	1874	1874	0	20534	18740	1794	44358	37480	6878	69925	56220	13705
OUTLAY AFTER TAX	1874	1874	0	18740	18740	0	37480	37480	0	56220	56220	0
LIQUIDATING VALUE	9435	10340	-905	23510	23980	-470	45876	40182	5694	83726	56300	27426
PROCEEDS FOR ESTATE	198595	100000	98595	182730	100000	82730	169394	100000	69394	172826	100000	72826

ANNUAL EARNING RATES OF EQUITIES IN CALCULATIONS
START # THROUGH · EQUITY · START # · THRU # · EQUITY
0% · 2005 · 0% · B · 0% · 2005 · 0%

	5-Q VALUE			TRUE COST/1000/YR @		
	PROPOSED	ORIGINAL	DIFFERENCE	PROPOSED	ORIGINAL	DIFFERENCE
	843. · 6077.	15658.	29863.	9.32	15.90	-6.58

Comments on Exhibit

The idea here is for solving the common problem of having additional needs for protection, but budget does not allow increased payments. By making more efficient use of money as stated earlier, this illustration shows how additional coverage can be obtained. As can be seen, the cost of the additional coverage is completely paid for by some of the future dividends of the existing policies, and yet most of the dividends are replaced by added cash value. Using future dividends to pay for protection needs today is an ideal solution, particularly in view of the fact that these future dividends are paid only if the insured lives for the period illustrated and the fact that if the insured can be certain that he or she will live, then the need for protection will no longer be necessary.

EXHIBIT 25.2
Excerpts from Promotional Brochures Describing the DISC System

Now, a new mini-computer system, DISC's Computer Analyzed Program, speedily prepares personalized in-depth proposals for you. These proposals help you demonstrate to your clients—factually and forcefully——how to put their hidden assets back to work for themselves. Moreover, these proposals help maximize tax savings from insurance for your clients—and help you demonstrate how to use those savings to maximize coverage.

Your mini-computer system will look like an attractive modern office desk with a typewriter on it. It takes up no more space than a simple office desk. Installation takes only a few hours and is handled by our specially trained personnel on your premises.

The computer helps eliminate human error to assure you of maximum accuracy. The printout is unusually neat, attractive, and easy to read. It's a pleasure to present to your client and it will enhance his or her view of your professionalism.

Moreover, unique to DISC's system are complete annual instructions for servicing your client effectively and conveniently. The instructions are broken down by policy and show you the insurance company, the client's premium and interest to be paid, as well as dividends, cash value loans, and tax savings to be reinvested.

The CAP educational and training program brings to insurance home offices and large agencies the only service of its kind in the insurance industry. Many proven tools used in the CAP program actually guarantee transferability. For example, the format of the DISC computer printout/case study presentation encourages effective selling and excellent communication between the agent and client.

Frankly, DISC's new mini-computer system is not designed for the average life insurance agent. Rather, it is designed especially to meet the needs of sophisticated, aggressive, already successful agents and agencies.

CASE 26

VOLKSWAGEN OF AMERICA
THE RABBIT

In January 1975, Volkswagen introduced the Rabbit to the American public. It was initially positioned as an automobile with "engineering advances that our competitors will not have for years to come." Introductory television and radio advertisements featured the musical theme of "Happy Days Are Here Again." Communications copy emphasized the Rabbit's styling, performance, and economy. In summary, it was offered as "The car of the future which is here today."

Four months after its introduction, sales for the Rabbit were well within Volkswagen's projections. Most purchasers rated its engineering very high and were pleased with its roominess. Concerns, however, were voiced over the gas mileage achieved and persistently squealing brakes. Since a price increase was inevitable due to changing economic conditions, Volkswagen was considering the best way to position the Rabbit consistent with the needs and attitudes of new car buyers.

Background Information

Ferdinant Porsche, a young automobile designer, initially developed the Volkswagen concept in the 1920's. He intended the car to be a completely

160

practical vehicle. At first, Porsche's plans for such an unconventional automobile were rejected by European automobile manufacturers. The rise of Hitler and his pledge to the German people that every man would own his own car, "The Volkswagen," stirred the implementation of Porsche's dream. The car's production, however, was disrupted by World War II.

After the war, British Occupational Forces controlled the Volkswagen factory until 1949. At that time the factory was turned over to Heinz Nordoff who faced the major task of rebuilding the Volkswagen organization. The basic design of the car, however, was not altered and engineering emphasis was directed toward internal improvements of the automobile.

Gradually a global sales and service organization developed. At present, Volkswagen A.G., located in Wolfsburg, is West Germany's largest industrial enterprise with factories located throughout the world.

Volkswagen sales in the United States peaked in 1970 at 582,500 cars, or about 7 percent of total U.S. sales. While imported automobiles expanded their share of the U.S. market as the 1970's continued, Volkswagen began to decline in market share and absolute sales. This decline came about because of the obvious increase in foreign car competition, the step-up of smaller car production by major U.S. manufacturers, and the prevailing economic conditions which resulted in more rapidly increasing prices for products imported from West Germany.

As part of the program designed to halt its declining market share, Volkswagen began to restructure its product line. In January 1974, Volkswagen introduced the Dasher (known in Europe as the Passat) to the United States. It was positioned as a totally different kind of Volkswagen. The Rabbit represented a continuation of Volkswagen's restructuring of its product line.

The Rabbit

The Rabbit, as shown in Exhibit 26.1, was designed by Giorgetto Giugiaro of Italy. It was engineered by Volkswagen to be a highly advanced yet practical car with a water-cooled, transverse-mounted, overhead-cam engine. Three models of the Rabbit were offered: the Basic Rabbit, the Custom Rabbit, and the Deluxe Rabbit. Both the custom and deluxe models were available with two or four doors, automatic or standard transmission, and a variety of optional equipment. The introductory suggested retail price of the Basic Rabbit was set at $2,999.

Specific features of the Rabbit can best be presented through the following copy extracted from an introductory, detailed information print advertisement titled, "Why Detroit's engineers are secretly praising Volkswagen's Rabbit."

One thing about the men of the engineering profession: they give credit where credit is due. Which may explain all the nice letters and phone calls we've received from Detroit since our new Rabbit has been out. Why all the praise?

93 miles per hour

A Rabbit is very fast. And although we obviously don't recommend 93 mph (please obey all speed limits), it is reassuring to know as you're about to get onto a hectic expressway, that a Rabbit has the power for great acceleration. From 0 to 50 in only 8.2 seconds. That's quicker than a Monza 2 + 2.

38 miles per gallon

A Rabbit is very thrifty. In the recent 1975-model Federal Environmental Protection Agency fuel economy tests, the Rabbit averaged 38 miles to the gallon on the highway. It averaged a nifty 24 in tougher stop-and-go city traffic.

As big inside as some mid-size cars

The Rabbit is a sub-compact sized car. That's on the outside. Open the door and it's a different story. 80 percent of the space in the car is devoted to functional room. There's actually more head and leg room inside than in some mid-size cars.

You get this feeling of roominess immediately, as you stretch out behind the wheel and look out through the huge front windshield. Visibility is incredible.

The main engineering feat that makes all this room possible is our revolutionary transverse engine, or stated more simply, an engine that is mounted sideways. Besides adding space, placing the engine in this manner, and slanting it, has a lot to do with why the Rabbit gets such good gas mileage. For now you have a very low silhouetted front end which means lower wind resistance, which means better gas mileage. The Rabbit comes only one way, as a Hatchback. And you don't pay a penny more for that extra door. In addition to the 2-door model shown, there is a 4-door available. Four doors plus a Hatchback. That's a lot of ins and outs in one car.

How we got it to handle so easily

The best way to describe driving a Rabbit is that it just *feels* right. The rack-and-pinion steering, designed exclusively for the Rabbit, allows you to feel in complete control especially on fast, right turns.

Another VW exclusive, an independent stabilizer rear axle, means independent wheel travel for more riding comfort and added safety on rough roads.

As is true on only two Detroit cars, the Eldorado and Toronado, the Rabbit has front-wheel drive for road-hugging ability. The firm and sporty ride of the car is enhanced by rigid shock rates and longer suspension travel.

Owner's Security Blanket[1]

To make sure your Rabbit lives a lively and a carefree life, it's backed by the most advanced car coverage plan in the automotive industry: The Volkswagen Owner's Security Blanket with exclusive Computer Analysis.

All for $2,999

[1]For a description of the Volkswagen Owner's Security Blanket, see Exhibit 26.2.

Lately, a lot of automotive executives have been giving speeches on "the car of the future." They see it as being small, low-priced, but with increased interior dimensions and more economical performance.

Ladies and gentlemen of the automotive industry, your car of the future, our Rabbit, is here today.

And it will only cost you $2,999 to try it out.

Happy days *are* here again.

Introduction of the Rabbit

The Rabbit was introduced in January 1975 with a national television and magazine campaign. Regional distributors and local dealers also supported the Rabbit's introduction via newspapers and radio as well as spot television. Examples of the introductory advertisements are shown in Exhibits 26.3, 26.4, and 26.5.

At the national level, about 70 percent of the introduction budget was allocated to television. Among the television shows utilized were "Sanford and Son," "Cannon," "Kojak," "The Waltons," and others. The national print effort included the major weekly and monthly publications. Special introduction and follow-up spreads were run in *TV Guide* and *Reader's Digest.* Introduction advertisements also appeared in special interest magazines with special market readers such as *Car & Driver, Road & Track, Playboy, Ebony, Black Enterprise, Tennis, Ski,* and others.

After the Rabbit had been introduced several magazines ran evaluations of the car and its performance. Selected quotes from these articles which were subsequently used by Volkswagen in its advertising for the Rabbit are shown in Exhibit 26.6.

Research on Rabbit Buyers

A mail survey was sent to 685 individuals who had purchased Rabbits during March of 1975. The questionnaire was designed to cover purchase criteria, other makes considered, alternative choice Volkswagen if the Rabbit were not available (i.e., substitution versus incremental sales), attitude and knowledge of Volkswagen salesmen, and value perceptions of the Rabbit. From the mail-out, 354 respondents returned the questionnaire and formed the basis of the selected results shown in Exhibit 26.7.

In another study a group of Rabbit buyers were compared with owners of other automobiles considered to be competitive with the Rabbit. Exhibit 26.8 indicates how Rabbit owners compare with owners of other automobiles on selected demographic variables.

EXHIBIT 26.1
The 1975 Volkswagen Rabbit

EXHIBIT 26.2
Description of Volkswagen Owner's Security Blanket

There's one area where the Rabbit will never get you in a stew. Repairs.

Under Volkswagen's Security Blanket for 12 months or 20,000 miles, whichever comes first, we'll fix or replace any part that's defective in materials or workmanship, except for filters, fluids, or regular maintenance services, free. Provided you exercise reasonable care and follow the VW maintenance schedule.

In addition, we warrant every internal engine and transmission part against defects in materials or workmanship for 24 months or 24,000 miles, whichever comes first.

What's more, if your car has to stay overnight for warranty repairs, if you've made an appointment you'll get something that'll help you keep your other appointments. Our car. Until yours is back on its feet.

And if your problem is minor, you shouldn't have a major wait. So we have an Express Care Service that handles problems that will take 30 minutes or less. In 30 minutes or less. While you wait.

In addition to this new car coverage, we have a 6 month/6,000 mile warranty covering parts and labor on all genuine VW parts used for repairs. And if your car is tied up for repairs not covered by the new car warranty, we can arrange to rent you one of our cars at a special rate, so you won't be tied up.

Now that you know what we do when we find trouble, you should also know that we can go looking for it.

Just bring your Volkswagen to our computer. We'll plug it in and it'll pour its heart out. With our computer analysis system, over 60 functions and components are checked.

EXHIBIT 26.3
Example of Introductory Print Advertisement

The 38mpg rabbit.

Happy days are here again.

Good news at last! Volkswagen *happily* introduces the Rabbit. The incredible new car that gets 38 highway miles per gallon and 24 in the city (according to the '75 model Federal EPA tests).

Good news travels fast, too. The Rabbit'll do 93 miles per hour (we strongly suggest you obey all speed limits) and has the power to scoot from 0 to 50 in just 8.2 seconds.

And, since the engine's mounted sideways, the sub-compact Rabbit has all the head and leg room of some mid-sized cars. It also has a hatchback, front-wheel drive, and VW's unique rear stabilizer axle.

All backed by the Volkswagen Owner's Security Blanket with Computer Analysis.††

See the new Volkswagen Rabbit. And ■ drive happily ever after.

ⓌⓌrabbit

Introducing the 93mph, 38mpg, $2999* VW rabbit.

*Suggested retail price Rabbit 2-door Hatchback, P.O.E. Local taxes, transportation and other delivery charges additional.
†† See your dealer for more details. ©Volkswagen of America, Inc.

Dealer Name

THIS AD AVAILABLE IN 5 SIZES:

	$2999	No Price
1000 lines	33-17-58470	33-17-58520
600 lines	33-17-58480	33-17-58530
400 lines	33-17-58490	33-17-58540
250 lines	33-17-58500	33-17-58550
150 lines	33-17-58510	33-17-58560

EXHIBIT 26.4
Storyboard for Introductory Television Commercial

18/2/3

PRODUCT: RABBIT
TITLE: "CAR WASH"

ORDER NO.: :30/:25 - VWRB-9283/93 (COMMON)
(NO PRICE)   :25 - VWRB-9343

1. (MUSIC THROUGHOUT) ANNCR: (VO) The incredible new Volkswagen Rabbit...

2. SINGERS: ...The skies above are clear again...

3. ANNCR: (VO) Averages 38 miles per gallon down the highway...

4. SINGERS: ...Happy days are here again.

5. ANNCR: (VO) Goes from 0 to 50

6. in a snappy 8.2 seconds...

7. Costs only twenty-nine, ninety nine...

8. And it's easy to wash.

9. SINGERS: Happy days are...

10. here again. (MUSIC OUT)

NOTE: VWRB-5143 (CALIFORNIA VERSION) HAS SUPER WHICH READS "$2999 SUGGESTED RETAIL PRICE. RABBIT 2-DOOR HATCH BACK, POE, TAXES, LICENSE, AND TRANSPORTATION CHARGES ADDITIONAL.

EXHIBIT 26.5
Example of Introductory Radio Commercial

Program: Volkswagen Radio
Product: Rabbit—Very Very Quick
Length: :50

"Happy Days" Music Gradually Building

ANNCR: If you're looking for a car that's very, very quick . . .
Yet gets very, very good gas mileage . . .
And doesn't cost very much at all . . .
Then happy days are here again!

That's right, Volkswagen *happily* introduces the Rabbit!
The 93-mile-per-hour . . . 38-mile-per-gallon . . . low-cost Volkswagen Rabbit!

93 miles per hour? We strongly suggest you obey all speed
limits, but you do have the power for incredible acceleration!
38 miles per gallon? Those are honest highway miles in the
'75 model EPA tests! It averaged 24 in the city. Low-cost?
Well, when you find out just how little a new Rabbit costs,
you're bound to agree that . . .
Happy Days are here again!

EXHIBIT 26.6
Selected Quotes from Articles about the Rabbit

Road & Track "This car does it all; it's small, light, roomy, and fast, with nimble and responsive steering, ride, and handling. Best sedan under $3,500."

Road Test Magazine. "It is the finest example to date of a totally integrated passenger car, useful anywhere in the world, and is qualified as no other imported car is for 1975 for the Road Test Engineering Award."

Popular Mechanics "Volkswagen's Rabbit is the best value for 1975."

Car & Driver "Whole populations of drivers will live for years with this car, strongly impressed by its generally nimble disposition and its sensitive feel of the road through the steering wheel and brake pedal."

Esquire "It is the specific type of car that Detroit will be building in the 1980's."

EXHIBIT 26.7
Selected Results from Survey of Rabbit Buyers

SOURCE OF FIRST AWARENESS OF RABBIT	Percentage
Advertising (Net)	47.7
Television	32.9
Newspaper	4.4
Time	3.0
Newsweek	1.7
Playboy	1.3
Other	4.4
Articles (Net)	17.1
Road & Track	3.7
Motor Trend	3.7
Popular Science	2.7
Car & Driver	2.0
Popular Mechanics	1.3
Other	3.7
At dealership	26.2
Through friends	8.0
On street	2.0

BODY STYLE, MODEL, AND OPTIONS	
Body Style	Percentage
Two-door	77.0
Four-door	23.0
	100.0
Model	
Price leader	9.3
Custom	36.7
Deluxe	54.0
	100.0
Option	
Passive belt	47.2
Rear window defogger	61.1
Air conditioning	17.3
Automatic transmission	15.0
Alloy wheels	11.6
Sunroof	5.3
AM radio	45.8
AM/FM radio	25.2

EXHIBIT 26.7 *(Continued)*

INITIAL REASON FOR CONSIDERING THE RABBIT
PRIOR TO VISITING DEALER

	Percentage
None–first saw at dealer	9.6
Economy (Net)	73.8
Gas mileage	58.5
Economy, generally	6.0
Price	6.3
38 mpg	2.0
Low maintenance costs	1.0
Styling (Net)	26.9
Roominess	11.7
Styling	7.3
Size	5.3
Hatchback	2.7
Engineering (Net)	26.2
Front wheel drive	15.9
Engineering	4.3
Water-cooled engine	3.7
Front engine	1.3
Rack and pinion steering	1.0
Performance (Net)	14.6
Pick-up	12.0
Handling	2.6
VW reputation	7.0
Previous VW experience	1.7

PREVIOUS VW/IMPORT
OWNERSHIP

	Percentage
Have never owned any imported car	21.2
Owned competitive imports only	15.8
	37.0
Previous VW owner	36.3
Reconquested VW owner	26.7
	100.0

VW MODEL WOULD HAVE PURCHASED
IF RABBIT NOT AVAILABLE

	Percentage
None	58.3
Beetle	19.4
Dasher	16.5
Wagon	2.9
Sirocco	1.4
Bus	1.1
"Thing"	.4
	100.0

EXHIBIT 26.7 *(Continued)*

EVALUATION OF SALESMAN

Primary Sales Points Made	Percentage
General	
Excellent gas mileage	30.7
Interior roominess	23.1
Great performance	25.6
Specific	
Front wheel drive	17.0
Rack and pinion steering	4.3
Transverse engine	1.8
Safety features	9.4
Warranty coverage	6.1
VW service	3.2
VW quality	6.1
Overall Opinion Of Salesman's Attitude Toward Rabbit	
Positive/enthusiastic/helpful	90.4
Poor knowledge/negative	9.6
	100.0

PRIMARY REASONS FOR PURCHASE

	Percentage
Gas economy	75.2
Roominess	30.2
Performance	29.2
Handling	19.1
Styling/Hatchback	19.1
Front wheel drive	14.1
Price	13.7
VW reputation	12.1
VW service	9.7
Comfort	7.0
VW quality	6.4
Test drive	3.7
Previous experience with VW	2.7

GASOLINE MILEAGE

Average Miles Per Gallon	More Than Expected	Less Than Expected	About Expected
26.3 mpg	6.8%	53.4%	39.8%

WHAT IS LIKED BEST

	Percentage
Economy/Gas mileage	45.8
Handling	48.6
Performance/Pick-up	38.1
Interior roominess	25.2
Comfort	15.4
Visibility	6.3
Styling	4.2
Front wheel drive	4.5
Everything	5.2

EXHIBIT 26.7 *(Continued)*

WHAT IS LIKED LEAST

	Percentage
Nothing	13.7
Brakes	18.9
Gas mileage	12.0
Quality	9.3
Seats	5.2
Engine noise	6.2
Interlock seat belts	3.4
Passive seat belts	3.8
Shifting difficulty (Can't find first)	8.2
Catalytic converter (Light goes on)	6.5
Gas pedal placement	5.5
Oil dip stick location	3.4
Rear window gets dirty	2.7

WHO WOULD RECOMMEND RABBIT TO OTHERS AND WHY (OR WHY NOT)

	Percentage
Would recommend Rabbit to others because of	89.8
Handling	7.1
Roominess	4.1
Value for money	4.1
All-round great car	4.4
Gas mileage	3.4
Fun	3.1
Would not recommend Rabbit to others because of	5.4
Gas mileage	1.7
Dealer service	1.4
Just don't recommend cars	.7
Mechanical problems	.7
Poor quality	.7
Hesitation/brakes	.7
Don't know yet if would recommend	4.8
	100.0

EXHIBIT 26.8
Demographic Characteristics of Rabbit Owners and Owners of Selected Other Automobiles

	RABBIT	TYPE 1	DATSUN B210	TOYOTA	PACER	GREMLIN	PINTO	VEGA
Male	76.6%	57.8%	72.2%	71.7%	70.1%	63.9%	71.1%	66.4%
Female	23.4	42.2	27.8	28.3	29.9	36.1	28.9	33.6
	100.0	100.0	100.0	100.0	100.0	100.0	100.0	100.0
Married	79.2	63.6	70.5	76.6	79.5	68.6	78.0	74.4
Single	17.5	30.4	24.5	20.5	15.2	26.0	17.1	22.1
Other	3.3	6.0	5.0	2.9	5.3	5.4	4.9	3.5
	100.0	100.0	100.0	100.0	100.0	100.0	100.0	100.0
Age								
Under 20	1.3	7.7	5.1	5.4	1.2	6.8	4.2	7.7
20–24	17.9	30.2	20.4	20.5	9.5	19.0	17.0	21.4
25–29	22.2	19.1	22.2	22.8	14.5	22.8	19.3	22.2
30–34	18.8	11.7	15.4	14.9	13.2	11.6	13.0	12.0
35–39	10.1	7.3	10.1	7.8	11.1	8.8	8.0	8.2
40–44	9.8	5.4	6.1	7.1	12.0	9.7	6.3	6.7
45–49	4.5	5.1	6.2	4.7	9.5	4.4	8.1	6.8
50–54	6.2	6.3	4.6	8.5	8.7	7.5	10.7	4.8
55–59	4.6	5.2	4.6	2.5	10.7	3.2	4.2	2.5
60–64	1.8	0.6	2.0	3.5	4.6	3.4	5.9	4.2
65 and over	2.8	1.4	3.3	2.3	5.0	2.8	3.3	3.5
	100.0	100.0	100.0	100.0	100.0	100.0	100.0	100.0
Median Age	32.3	28.2	30.7	30.4	40.2	30.6	33.6	29.7
Education								
Some high school or less	3.4	7.2	9.9	5.1	3.7	6.5	9.0	8.7
High school graduate	16.8	25.8	23.9	23.3	28.9	29.6	27.2	29.4
Some college	30.4	39.4	28.9	28.8	34.0	37.9	31.7	30.6
College graduate	18.8	19.9	22.1	22.3	14.0	15.1	15.3	16.6
Some post graduate study	13.7	3.8	6.5	8.9	9.9	5.9	6.9	6.5
Post graduate degree	16.9	3.9	8.7	11.6	9.5	5.0	9.9	8.2
	100.0	100.0	100.0	100.0	100.0	100.0	100.0	100.0

EXHIBIT 26.8 (Continued)

Occupation								
Professional	38.0	26.6	26.8	31.7	30.3	22.9	22.9	22.6
Skilled craftsman	10.1	10.7	11.2	8.1	8.8	15.0	10.7	8.3
Managerial	9.8	5.3	11.6	14.0	15.0	13.5	8.0	10.8
Retired	6.8	2.4	5.7	4.5	9.2	4.4	5.6	5.0
Public service	5.6	5.1	7.0	5.6	4.2	3.5	7.2	4.5
Clerical	5.3	14.5	8.8	8.1	5.4	13.5	8.0	10.8
Military	5.3	5.5	5.8	3.9	2.1	3.8	6.5	5.8
Student	5.2	8.8	6.9	3.6	1.7	6.8	3.8	6.5
Laborer	5.2	5.7	7.2	6.0	5.0	9.1	8.8	8.0
Housewife	3.2	2.6	2.8	5.0	7.1	4.6	9.2	5.4
Other	5.5	12.3	6.2	9.5	11.2	2.9	9.3	12.3
	100.0	100.0	100.0	100.0	100.0	100.0	100.0	100.0
Income								
Under $5,000	.7	4.2	4.0	3.0	1.3	5.7	4.1	5.1
$5,001–$7,500	4.4	8.6	6.4	4.6	3.4	7.4	5.9	7.6
$7,501–$8,500	3.9	1.5	4.1	6.3	3.8	7.4	9.6	4.2
$8,501–$10,000	7.9	8.9	6.7	9.8	6.0	10.5	9.6	11.1
$10,001–$12,500	14.7	13.2	9.9	12.4	5.5	13.8	12.1	11.7
$12,501–$15,000	13.3	10.9	13.4	13.3	14.9	12.5	12.2	12.3
$15,001–$20,000	22.2	23.1	25.5	20.6	23.0	21.2	22.9	22.3
$20,001–$25,000	12.6	14.8	15.2	14.0	17.8	8.9	12.5	12.1
$25,001–$30,000	7.8	6.4	7.6	8.1	11.5	6.6	2.5	5.1
$30,001–$35,000	5.0	3.6	2.2	2.5	4.7	2.7	3.7	3.4
$35,001–$40,000	3.2	—	1.4	2.1	1.3	0.7	1.0	3.0
Over $40,000	3.9	4.8	2.9	3.3	6.8	2.6	3.9	1.8
N/A	0.4	—	0.9	—	—	—	—	0.3
	100.0	100.0	100.0	100.0	100.0	100.0	100.0	100.0
Median Income	$16,249	$15,929	$15,934	$15,194	$18,291	$13,544	$14,289	$14,559

SOURCE: Rogers National Research, Inc.

ANALYSIS FORM

Case 1

Wendy's International, Inc. (A)

1. What do you see as the "real business" of Wendy's?

_____

_____

_____

_____

_____

_____

_____

2. What are the basic reasons that people patronize fast food restaurants?

_____

_____

_____

_____

_____

_____

_____

_____

_____

3. Based upon the concentric circles shown here, how would you describe the competition for Wendy's? Describe each circle as a level of competition moving from the closest (B) to the furthest (E) away from Wendy's.

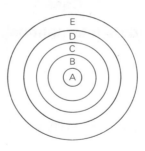

A. Wendy's _____

B. _____

C. _____

D. _____

E. _____

4. Wendy's philosophy is to direct the promotion, motif, and product toward the adult market, and through the adult, get the family trade. Do you agree with this philosophy? Why or why not?

_____

_____

_____

_____

_____

_____

_____

_____

_____

5. Discuss the relative advantages and disadvantages of using the seemingly more labor-intensive method of preparing every hamburger to order versus precooking and prewrapping.

ADVANTAGES	DISADVANTAGES

6. What types of marketing research would be helpful to Wendy's at this point in time?

_____

_____

_____

_____

_____

_____

_____

_____

_____

_____

_____

_____

_____

7. Compare the Wendy's pick-up customer with the one who eats on the premises. What communications appeals should be used to reach each of these customers?

Pick-up Customer: _____

_____

_____

_____

_____

On Premises Diner: _____

_____

_____

_____

17·8

ANALYSIS FORM

Case 2

Pepsi-Cola Company

1. If the majority of consumers really like the taste of Pepsi more than the taste of Coke, why don't more of them purchase Pepsi?

_____

_____

_____

_____

_____

_____

_____

_____

2. What recommendations would you make to Coca-Cola in terms of responding to the Pepsi Challenge? Support your recommendations.

_____

_____

_____

_____

_____

_____

3. What do you see as the relative advantages and disadvantages of a national versus a localized Pepsi Challenge advertising campaign?

NATIONAL CAMPAIGN	LOCALIZED CAMPAIGN
Advantages	*Advantages*
Disadvantages	*Disadvantages*

4. Based on your analysis in the above matrix do you believe that Pepsi should go national with the Challenge campaign? Why or why not?

_____

_____

_____

_____

_____

_____

_____

_____

_____

180

5. Discuss other types of research that might be helpful to Pepsi at this time.

_____

_____

_____

_____

_____

_____

_____

_____

_____

_____

6. Discuss comparative advertisements in general in terms of reasons for and reasons against their use.

Reasons For: _____

_____

_____

_____

_____

_____

Reasons Against: _____

_____

_____

_____

_____

_____

181

7. What do you see as the long-run impact of comparative advertising campaigns such as the Pepsi Challenge?

_____

_____

_____

_____

_____

_____

_____

_____

_____

ANALYSIS FORM

Case 3

Harper Bank

1. Based on your analysis of the case what do you see as the basic problem facing Harper Bank at this time?

_____

_____

_____

_____

_____

_____

_____

2. Discuss the marketing concept as it might be applied to a "goods-producing firm" and a "services-producing firm" such as a bank.

GOODS-PRODUCING FIRM	SERVICES-PRODUCING FIRM (BANK)

3. Why do you believe the application of the marketing concept to the Harper Bank was not successful?

_____

_____

_____

_____

_____

_____

_____

_____

_____

4. What are some of the basic reasons as to why a consumer chooses one financial institution over another?

_____

_____

_____

_____

_____

_____

_____

_____

_____

5. Discuss ways in which a bank can be more responsive to the needs of its consumers.

_____

_____

_____

_____

_____

_____

_____

_____

6. What types of marketing research would be helpful to Harper Bank at this time? How would you conduct the needed research?

_____

_____

_____

_____

_____

_____

_____

_____

_____

7. Based on your problem statement in question 1, what specific recommendations would you make to the management of Harper Bank?

_____

_____

_____

_____

_____

_____

_____

_____

_____

_____

_____

_____

_____

_____

_____

_____

_____

ANALYSIS FORM

Case 4
Honeywell

1. Do you believe there is a market for fire and smoke detectors today? Why or why not?

_____

_____

_____

_____

_____

_____

_____

2. Describe the socioeconomic and demographic characteristics of consumers most likely to be in the market for Honeywell's detector.

_____

_____

_____

_____

_____

_____

_____

_____

_____

3. What basic communication appeals could be used to reach these prospective consumers?

_____

_____

_____

_____

_____

_____

_____

_____

_____

_____

4. Explain how the following elements of marketing's environment have already or could in the future affect the demand for fire and smoke detectors.

LEGAL-POLITICAL	ECONOMIC
COMPETITIVE	SOCIETAL-CULTURAL

5. Evaluate the following media choices for communicating with prospective consumers for Honeywell's detector.

Newspapers: _____

_____

Direct Mail: _____

_____

Radio: _____

_____

Point of Purchase: _____

_____

Television: _____

_____

6. List four types of possible retail outlets for Honeywell's detector and discuss the strengths and weaknesses of each.

RETAIL OUTLET	WEAKNESSES	STRENGTHS

189

7. Based on your analysis list your specific recommendations (and supporting rationale) to Honeywell for each of the following decision issues:

Target Consumers to Reach: _____

    Rationale: _____

_____

Promotion Appeals to Use: _____

    Rationale: _____

_____

Media to Reach Consumers: _____

    Rationale: _____

_____

Retail Outlets to Use: _____

    Rationale: _____

_____

ANALYSIS FORM

Case 5

Tuller Fruit Farm (A)

1. In terms of consumer behavior how would you describe the real business of Tuller Fruit Farm?

_____

_____

_____

_____

_____

_____

_____

_____

2. Using the following matrix, describe the segments of consumers who are likely to patronize an establishment like Tuller's and then indicate each segment's motivation for such shopping behavior.

DESCRIPTION OF MARKET SEGMENTS	CONSUMER MOTIVATIONS

3. In addition to the items described in the case what other types of products or services should Tuller's consider to maintain its growth?

_____

_____

_____

_____

_____

_____

_____

_____

4. How price sensitive or price conscious would you say that Tuller's customers are? Why do you say that?

_____

_____

_____

_____

_____

_____

_____

_____

_____

_____

5. Evaluate Tuller's current position on promotion. What changes, if any, do you recommend? Why?

_____

_____

_____

_____

_____

_____

_____

_____

_____

_____

6. What do you project as the future for firms like Tuller's? Why?

_____

_____

_____

_____

_____

_____

_____

_____

_____

_____

_____

7. What types of marketing recommendations would you make to Tuller's in terms of coping with the future?

_____

_____

_____

_____

_____

_____

_____

_____

_____

_____

_____

_____

_____

_____

_____

_____

_____

_____

ANALYSIS FORM

Case 6

Canadian Automobile Association

1. What bases would you utilize to segment the market for memberships in the Canadian Automobile Association?

_____

_____

_____

_____

_____

_____

_____

_____

2. What approaches would you recommend as possible ways to reduce membership turnover?

_____

_____

_____

_____

_____

_____

_____

3. Compare the three common methods of gathering consumer survey data in terms of the four trade-offs in any marketing research project.

TRADE-OFFS	TELEPHONE SURVEY	MAIL SURVEY	PERSONAL SURVEY
Time			
Cost			
Quality of Data			
Quantity of Data			

4. What do you see as the specific objectives that should be accomplished in the consumer research for the ECC?

_____

_____

_____

_____

_____

_____

_____

_____

_____

5. Discuss the types of marketing data that should be gathered to meet the research objectives.

_____

_____

_____

_____

_____

_____

_____

_____

_____

_____

197

6. Specifically, what method of survey research would you use to gather the needed consumer data? Why?

_____

_____

_____

_____

_____

_____

_____

_____

7. In the following spaces give specific examples of the ways in which you would ask the questions to obtain the desired data of question 5.

_____

_____

_____

_____

_____

_____

_____

_____

_____

_____

_____

ANALYSIS FORM

Case 7

Libb Pharmaceuticals

1. What do you see as the basic problem facing Libb Pharmaceuticals at this time?

_____

_____

_____

_____

_____

_____

_____

2. In the following matrix indicate how the four basic determinants of consumer behavior are involved in brand preference for toothpaste.

NEEDS	MOTIVES
PERCEPTION	ATTITUDES

3. Indicate the impact that each of the following influences may have on the selection of a brand of toothpaste.

Social Influences: _____

_____

_____

Family Influences: _____

_____

_____

Cultural Influences: _____

_____

_____

4. Evaluate the research methodology used by Libb in studying the toothpaste market. In what ways could the research have been strengthened?

_____

_____

_____

_____

_____

_____

_____

_____

_____

_____

_____

_____

_____

5. What other types of analyses could have been done on the data?

_____

_____

_____

_____

_____

_____

_____

_____

_____

6. What other types of research should Libb consider undertaking on the toothpaste market?

_____

_____

_____

_____

_____

_____

_____

_____

_____

7. Based on your response to question 1 indicate the specific recommendations you would make to Libb Pharmaceuticals at this time.

ANALYSIS FORM

Case 8

General Consumer Appliances

1. Why do so many of the products that are introduced each year fail?

_____

_____

_____

_____

_____

_____

_____

_____

_____

_____

2. For each of the stages in the product life cycle cite an appliance that is currently in that stage and briefly explain why it is there.

STAGE	APPLIANCE	REASONS THE APPLIANCE IS IN THE STAGE
Introduction		
Growth		
Maturity		
Decline		

3. For the following emerging lifestyles indicate possible new product opportunities for General Consumer Appliances and briefly state what marketing appeals you would use to reach potential consumers for the products.

LIFESTYLE	PRODUCT OPPORTUNITIES	MARKETING APPEALS TO REACH CONSUMERS
New Theology of Pleasure		
Life Simplification		
Changing Femininity		
Appearance and Health		
Novelty, Change, and Escape		
Personal Creativity		
Energy Conservation		

204

4. For the following emerging lifestyles indicate how General Consumer Appliances might incorporate the lifestyle into its communications strategy for the firm's existing small appliances.

LIFESTYLE	WAYS TO INCORPORATE INTO COMMUNICATIONS STRATEGY
Instant Gratification	
Morality Revolution	
Familism Trends	
Youth Orientation	
Consumerism	

205

5. What do you see as some of the changes that are likely to occur in the elements of the cultural transfusive triad in the future?

Family: _____

_____

_____

_____

Church: _____

_____

_____

_____

School: _____

_____

_____

_____

6. Discuss ways that a firm like General Consumer Appliances could keep aware of the changing values and emerging lifestyles of consumers.

_____

_____

_____

_____

_____

_____

_____

_____

_____

206

ANALYSIS FORM

Case 9

Life Restaurant

1. How would you describe the "real business" of Life Restaurant? What really is its product?

_____

_____

_____

_____

_____

_____

_____

2. Discuss the target customer of Life Restaurant in terms of sex, education, age, income, and lifestyle.

_____

_____

_____

_____

_____

_____

_____

207

3. What implications does the observed tendency toward more meals being eaten away from home have for Life Restaurant and its basic philosophy?

_____

_____

_____

_____

_____

_____

_____

_____

_____

4. How do you see Life Restaurant positioned vis-a-vis vegetarian restaurants, which claim a similar philosophy?

_____

_____

_____

_____

_____

_____

_____

5. Discuss possible marketing strategies which could be used for moving people through the stages of the consumer adoption process for Life Restaurant.

STAGES	MARKETING STRATEGIES
Awareness	
Interest	
Evaluation	
Trial	
Adoption	

209

6. What types of marketing research do you think Life Restaurant should undertake?

_____

_____

_____

_____

_____

_____

_____

_____

7. What specific recommendations would you make to the organizers of Life Restaurant? Provide justification for your recommendations.

_____

_____

_____

_____

_____

_____

_____

_____

_____

_____

_____

_____

ANALYSIS FORM

Case 10

Dow Chemical Company

1. What do you see as the basic problem facing the marketers of Dow Domes at this time?

_____

_____

_____

_____

_____

_____

_____

_____

_____

_____

2. What alternative markets are open to Dow Chemical for its domes?

_____

_____

_____

_____

_____

_____

_____

3. Discuss possible marketing strategies which could be used for moving potential customers through the stages of the adoption process as applied to Dow Domes.

STAGES	MARKETING STRATEGIES
Awareness	
Interest	
Evaluation	
Trial	
Adoption	

4. How can Dow best reach and cultivate the most promising market (in your opinion) from those you presented in question 2?

_____

_____

_____

_____

_____

_____

_____

_____

_____

_____

5. What are the potential advantages and disadvantages associated with a firm typing all of its products together under one corporate name (e.g., Dow Domes)?

Advantages: _____

_____

_____

_____

_____

Disadvantages: _____

_____

_____

_____

213

6. What strategy should Dow employ in dealing with competitors who attempt to market a somewhat lower quality product (at a lower price) as an equal to its Domes?

_____

_____

_____

_____

_____

_____

_____

_____

_____

_____

7. Based on your overall analysis of the case and consistent with your response to question 1 what specific recommendations would you make to Dow?

_____

_____

_____

_____

_____

_____

_____

_____

ANALYSIS FORM

Case 11

JS&A National Sales Group

1. What are some of the basic reasons as to why this form of retailing is successful today when it probably would have not been so 10 or 20 years ago?

_____

_____

_____

_____

_____

_____

_____

_____

_____

2. Discuss how JS&A's approach to retailing could be thought of as possibly descriptive of all three major strategies of distribution.

Intensive: _____

_____

Selective: _____

_____

Exclusive: _____

_____

215

3. What other types of products would lend themselves to a pattern of distribution and promotion as used by JS&A?

_____

_____

_____

_____

_____

_____

_____

4. Discuss other forms of communications that could be used by JS&A to promote its products.

_____

_____

_____

_____

_____

_____

_____

_____

_____

_____

_____

_____

5. In terms of the following alternative retail outlets for PocketCom, discuss the possible advantages and disadvantages of each.

RETAIL OUTLETS	POSSIBLE ADVANTAGES	POSSIBLE DISADVANTAGES
Electronic Stores		
Discount Stores		
Department Stores		
JS&A		

6. What do you see as possible problems that JS&A may face in the next five
   to ten years?

   _____

   _____

   _____

   _____

   _____

   _____

   _____

   _____

7. What specific marketing recommendations would you make to JS&A at this
   time and for the future?

   _____

   _____

   _____

   _____

   _____

   _____

   _____

   _____

   _____

   _____

ANALYSIS FORM

Case 12

Simpson's Food Warehouse

1. Discuss the impact that each of the following environmental factors is having on the traditional supermarket today.

FACTOR	IMPACT UPON SUPERMARKETS
Cultural and Social Environment	
Legal and Political Environment	
Competitive Environment	
Economic Environment	

2. What are the basic criteria that consumers use to choose one retail food
   outlet over another?

_____

_____

_____

_____

_____

_____

_____

_____

3. What segment of consumers would most likely be attracted to a firm like
   Simpson's? Describe these consumers in as much detail as you can.

_____

_____

_____

_____

_____

_____

_____

_____

_____

_____

4. What are the potential advantages and disadvantages to Simpson's in the use of a membership fee to be able to shop at the store?

Advantages: _____

_____

_____

_____

Disadvantages: _____

_____

_____

_____

5. Should Simpson's seek to cut costs further by totally eliminating the relatively labor-intensive meat and product departments? Discuss the ramification of such a move.

_____

_____

_____

_____

_____

_____

_____

_____

_____

_____

_____

_____

221

6. What types of marketing research would be helpful to Simpson's at this time?

_____

_____

_____

_____

_____

_____

_____

_____

7. Based on your analysis of the case what specific recommendations would you make to Simpson's at this time?

_____

_____

_____

_____

_____

_____

_____

_____

_____

_____

_____

_____

_____

_____

ANALYSIS FORM

Case 13

Hyde-Phillip Chemical Company

1. Using the following matrix, discuss the general advantages and disadvantages associated with using each of the given forms of sales representation.

FORM OF REPRESENTATION	ADVANTAGES	DISADVANTAGES
Company Sales Force		
Merchant Wholesaler		
Agent Wholesaler		

2. After filling in the following cross tabulation form discuss the relationship between level of sales and geographic location.

Relationship: _____

_____

_____

_____

_____

_____

_____

_____

_____

_____

_____

_____

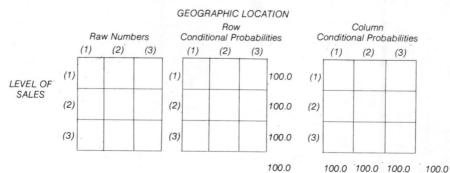

3. After filling in the following two cross-tabulation forms discuss the relationship between use of sales support and type of distribution and sales.

   Relationship: _____

   _____

   _____

   _____

   _____

   _____

   _____

   _____

   _____

   _____

   _____

USE OF SALES SUPPORT

		Raw Numbers			Row Conditional Proababilities				Column Conditional Probabilities		
		(1)	(2)	(3)	(1)	(2)	(3)		(1)	(2)	(3)
LEVEL OF SALES	(1)							100.0 (1)			
	(2)							100.0 (2)			
	(3)							100.0 (3)			
							100.00		100.0	100.0	100.0	100.0

USE OF SALES SUPPORT

		Raw Numbers			Row Conditional Probabilities				Column Conditional Probabilities		
		(1)	(2)	(3)	(1)	(2)	(3)		(1)	(2)	(3)
TYPE OF REPRESEN-TATION	(1)							100.0 (1)			
	(2)							100.0 (2)			
	(3)							100.00 (3)			
							100.0		100.0	100.0	100.0	100.0

4. What other types of information would assist Claxton in evaluating forms of
   sales representation?

   _____

   _____

   _____

   _____

   _____

   _____

   _____

   _____

5. What would be your specific recommendations to Hyde-Phillip at this time?

   _____

   _____

   _____

   _____

   _____

   _____

   _____

   _____

   _____

   _____

   _____

ANALYSIS FORM

Case 14

Youngs Drug Products

1. For years the topic of whether marketing is adaptive or formative has been discussed. Using this case as a focus discuss the adaptive aspect of marketing in terms of what changes in our cultural and social environment have brought about the changing attitudes toward sex and birth control. Then discuss the formative aspect of marketing in terms of what changes in our cultural and social environment are being brought about or could be brought about by increased advertising for contraceptives.

ADAPTIVE ASPECTS	FORMATIVE ASPECTS

227

2. Should advertising themes for contraceptives be aimed at females, males, or both? Why?

_____

_____

_____

_____

_____

_____

_____

_____

3. Should advertising themes for contraceptives focus on family planning, medical consideration, and/or other types of messages? Why?

_____

_____

_____

_____

_____

_____

_____

_____

_____

4. Contrast "hard sell" versus "soft sell" advertising in the context of this case.

Hard Sell: _____

_____

_____

Soft Sell: _____

_____

_____

5. Outline the basic reasons for and those against allowing contraceptive advertising on television.

REASONS FOR	REASONS AGAINST

6. In your objective opinion, should advertising for contraceptives be allowed on television? Why or why not?

_____

_____

_____

_____

_____

_____

_____

_____

_____

_____

7. Based on your analysis of the case what specific recommendations would you make to Youngs Drug? Support your recommendations by providing your rationale.
   Specific Recommendations: _____

_____

_____

_____

_____

   Rationale for Recommendations: _____

_____

_____

_____

ANALYSIS FORM

Case 15

International Telephone and Telegraph

1. In your own words what would you describe as the basic objective of ITT's corporate advertising program? Do you agree that this is what the objective should be? Why or why not?

_____

_____

_____

_____

_____

_____

_____

2. In what ways could ITT's corporate advertising be related to the following types of institutional advertising?
   Informative Institutional Advertising: _____

_____

_____

   Persuasive Institutional Advertising: _____

_____

_____

   Reminder-oriented Institutional Advertising: _____

_____

_____

231

3. Discuss the relative advantages and disadvantages of the following media for ITT's corporate advertising:

MEDIA	ADVANTAGES	DISADVANTAGES
Print		
Radio		
Television		

4. For the three television storyboards given in Exhibit 15.1 indicate what is trying to be communicated and how well you believe the message is getting through. Please support your response to the second part of the question.

COMMERCIAL	COMMUNICATION	HOW WELL IT IS GETTING THROUGH
Night Blindness		
Heart Mannequin		
Fellowships		

233

5. Discuss the specifics of other types of research you feel ITT should undertake at this point.

_____

_____

_____

_____

_____

_____

_____

_____

6. Discuss other types of themes you feel would be appropriate for ITT's corporate advertising program. Support your recommendations.

_____

_____

_____

_____

_____

_____

_____

_____

_____

_____

_____

ANALYSIS FORM

Case 16

Allegheny Airlines

1. What is the "real business" of Allegheny Airlines?

_____

_____

2. Based on your analysis of the case and the supporting exhibits please indicate in your own words what you perceive to be the major communications problem facing Allegheny today.

_____

_____

3. Two basic types of travelers are discretionary (traveling because they want to, i.e., for pleasure or vacation) and nondiscretionary (traveling because they need to, i.e., for business or personal problems). In the following matrix please list in the rows some of the reasons a person might choose to travel on one airline over another. Then for each of the columns place a number from 1 to 5 which indicates your perception of the importance of that reason for each type of traveler. Place a "1" if you think the reason is very important, "5" if very unimportant, or somewhere in between depending on the relative importance.

| REASONS FOR SELECTING AN AIRLINE | IMPORTANCE FOR TYPES OF TRAVELERS | |
	DISCRETIONARY	NONDISCRETIONARY

235

4. Discuss the potential advantages and disadvantages of naming one's competitors in an advertising program.

Advantages: _____

_____

_____

Disadvantages: _____

_____

_____

_____

_____

_____

5. Discuss the ways one could pretest and posttest the effectiveness of Allegheny's advertising program.

Pretest: _____

_____

_____

Posttest: _____

_____

_____

_____

_____

_____

236

6. Indicate how Allegheny's current advertising campaign meets each of the following possible objectives for a promotional program.

OBJECTIVE	HOW ALLEGHENY'S CURRENT CAMPAIGN MEETS THE OBJECTIVE
Provide Information	
Stimulus Demand	
Differentiate the Product	
Accentuate the Value of the Product	
Stabilize Sales	

237

7. What changes, if any, would you recommend in Allegheny's advertising program? Support your recommendations based on your overall analysis of the case and your response to question 2.

Recommendations: _____

_____

_____

_____

Rationale: _____

_____

_____

_____

_____

_____

_____

_____

_____

_____

_____

238

ANALYSIS FORM

Case 17

Tuller Fruit Farm (B)

1. Do you agree with the strategy of selling an 8-ounce glass of orange juice for 20 cents and a 12-ounce glass for 30 cents? Why or why not?

_____

_____

_____

_____

_____

_____

_____

2. Explain how Tuller's might use the concept of "psychological pricing" for the fresh orange juice.

_____

_____

_____

_____

_____

_____

_____

_____

3. If you were going to use a full costing approach to the pricing of the orange juice what would be the fixed costs and the variable costs that you would have to take into account?

Fixed Costs: _____

_____

_____

_____

_____

Variable Costs: _____

_____

_____

_____

_____

4. If Tuller's desired a 50 percent markup on orange juice how much would have to be added to the variable costs to come up with the selling price?

_____

_____

_____

_____

_____

_____

_____

_____

5. Based on the data in the case and the following assumptions calculate how many gallons of orange juice a year would have to be sold at $4.00/gallon in order to break even. Assume life of the machine is 5 years, annual maintenance is $25, and that it takes about 75 cents in labor costs to obtain a gallon of orange juice. Show your work in the following spaces:

Variable costs/gallon = _____

_____

_____

_____

_____

_____

_____

_____

_____

_____

_____

_____

_____

_____

_____

_____

_____

6. What prices would you recommend that Tuller's charge for the four sizes of orange juice it sells? Justify your recommendations.

_____

_____

_____

_____

_____

_____

_____

_____

_____

_____

_____

_____

_____

_____

_____

_____

_____

_____

ANALYSIS FORM

Case 18

Jai Lai Restaurant

1. Discuss the impact of the following environmental influences upon the restaurant industry today.

INFLUENCE	IMPACT UPON RESTAURANT INDUSTRY
Social and Cultural Environment	
Economic Environment	
Competitive Environment	

2. Discuss the concept of marginal pricing as it applies to this case. What does it mean?

_____

_____

_____

_____

_____

_____

_____

_____

_____

3. What are the relative advantages and disadvantages of each of the following forms of price promotion?

Coupon Program: _____

_____

_____

_____

Discount Program: _____

_____

_____

_____

Rebate Program: _____

_____

_____

4. Do you agree with the logic behind Jai Lai's rebate program as presented in the case? Why or why not?

_____

_____

_____

_____

_____

_____

_____

_____

_____

5. What other types of promotion other than price could be used to attract additional customers during the week day evenings?

_____

_____

_____

_____

_____

_____

_____

_____

_____

_____

245

6. Should the rebate program be continued? Support your conclusions with financial considerations. Should any changes be made in the program?

COMPUTATIONS:

Recommendations: _____

_____

_____

_____

_____

_____

_____

_____

_____

_____

_____

ANALYSIS FORM

Case 19

Haire Brothers Funeral Chapel

1. Using the model of profitability given in Worksheet 19.1 compute the return-of-net-worth (RONW) before taxes for Haire Brothers Funeral Chapel in 1976. What are the various ways which could be used to improve this RONW?

_____

_____

_____

_____

_____

_____

2. Discuss what you believe would be an appropriate ROI before taxes for a funeral firm. Why?

_____

_____

_____

_____

_____

_____

3. Discuss what you believe would be an appropriate markup for funeral merchandise such as caskets, vaults, and clothing.

_____

_____

_____

_____

_____

_____

_____

_____

4. Using your responses to questions 2 and 3 and the information in the case complete the ROI approach to determining prices as shown in Worksheet 19.2. Indicate the methodology you would use to break down the price determined in Worksheet 19.2 into more detail for a professional or itemized approach to pricing.

_____

_____

_____

_____

_____

_____

_____

_____

_____

ANALYSIS FORM

Case 20

Campus Crusade for Christ International

1. What is the "real product" being offered and the "consumer need" being satisfied by Campus Crusade for Christ?

   Real Product: _____

   _____

   _____

   Consumer Need: _____

   _____

   _____

2. Discuss ways and give examples of how the marketing objectives could be made more specific for the Here's Life, America campaign.

   _____

   _____

   _____

   _____

   _____

   _____

   _____

   _____

   _____

   _____

   _____

3. For each of the following marketing terms indicate what the term means in general and specifically how it is applicable in this case study.

MARKETING TERM	WHAT IT MEANS	ITS APPLICABILITY HERE
Market Segmentation		
Push-Pull Strategy		
Adoption Process		
Lifestyles		
Channels of Distribution		
Marketing Mix		

4. What approaches would you use to measure and evaluate the overall effectiveness of the Here's Life, America campaign?

_____

_____

_____

_____

_____

_____

_____

_____

_____

_____

5. Do you believe it is appropriate for religious organizations to use "marketing techniques"? Why or why not?

_____

_____

_____

_____

_____

_____

_____

_____

_____

_____

255

6. Based on your analysis of this case what specific marketing recommendations would you make for the Here's Life, America campaign? Discuss your rationale for these recommendations:

Marketing Recommendations: _____

_____

_____

_____

_____

_____

Rationale for Recommendations: _____

_____

_____

_____

_____

ANALYSIS FORM

Case 21

U.S. Postal Service

1 What would you define as the basic problems facing the U.S. Postal Service today?

_____

_____

_____

_____

_____

_____

_____

2. Describe and discuss the environmental changes in our society which have brought about the decline in household correspondence.

_____

_____

_____

_____

_____

_____

_____

257

3. Discuss the basic reasons why the USPS should advertise and why it should not advertise.

REASONS USPS SHOULD ADVERTISE	REASONS USPS SHOULD NOT ADVERTISE

258

4. In the following matrix several approaches to segmenting the market for household correspondence are presented. For each segment describe an appropriate advertising appeal and media-mix to reach that segment.

MARKET SEGMENTS	COMMUNICATION APPEALS	MEDIA MIX
Age Under 30		
30–50		
Over 50		
Sex Female		
Male		
Residence Urban		
Suburban		
Rural		

259

5. Based on your problem statements in question 1, what are your specific recommendations for the USPS? Also discuss your reasoning behind your recommendations.

Specific Recommendations: _____

_____

_____

_____

_____

_____

_____

_____

_____

Rationale for Recommendations: _____

_____

_____

_____

_____

_____

_____

_____

_____

_____

_____

_____

260

**The gift of a letter.
Nothing brings you closer to someone special.**

Remember how exciting it was to get a letter when you were young...especially if it was from your grandmother?

That's one thing that hasn't changed. A letter has always brought you close to the people you love.

That's because a letter or card is really a gift of yourself. A gift that lets people know what's on your mind. And in your heart.

Sometime soon, give someone special the gift of a letter. Nothing brings you closer to them.

P.S. Write Soon

1. How might you pretest the effectiveness of this advertisement?

_____

_____

_____

_____

_____

_____

2. Toward what market targets is this advertisement aimed?

_____

_____

_____

_____

_____

_____

3. Evaluate the creative appeal of this advertisement.

_____

_____

_____

_____

_____

4. Specifically, in what magazines would you place this advertisement and why?

_____

_____

_____

_____

_____

262

U.S. POSTAL SERVICE
"PREGNANT COUPLE"
Product: First Class-Household Correspondence

Length: 30 Seconds

Comm'l No.: UPFC 5613

MAN: Honey...it's your folks!

ANNCR: (VO) There's a gift that brings you close to someone special.

So close, you're right there with them...it's a letter.

WOMAN: (READING) "...talking about you again at breakfast. And we know your baby will be just as pretty as you were."

It's Mother's first picture of me.
MAN: It looks just like you.

WOMAN: (READING) "...if you need anything..."

ANNCR: (VO) The gift of a letter. Nothing brings you closer.

MAN: She says we can keep the picture...if we send one back! (LAUGHTER)

ANNCR: (VO) P.S. Write soon.

263

1. How might you pretest the effectiveness of this advertisement?

_____

_____

_____

_____

_____

2. Toward what market targets is this advertisement aimed?

_____

_____

_____

_____

3. Evaluate the creative appeal of this advertisement.

_____

_____

_____

_____

4. Specifically, on what types of television shows would you place this advertisement and why?

_____

_____

_____

_____

264

4. From the research results provided, fill in the following matrix:

ATTRIBUTE	IMPORTANCE TO CONSUMER	RANK OF COMPETING CHAINS ON ATTRIBUTE			
		WENDY'S	McDON-ALD'S	BURGER KING	BURGER CHEF
Taste of food Cleanliness Convenience Low cost menu Speed of service Popularity with children Variety of menu	1.56	2	1	3	4

aˉ The lower the attribute score the more important it is perceived.

5. From the matrix in question 4 discuss the image of Wendy's in relationship to the other three firms.

_____

_____

_____

_____

_____

_____

_____

_____

_____

_____

_____

_____

_____

_____

6. Based on these results suggest specific ways in which Wendy's might improve its consumer image vis-à-vis the other firms.

7. Evaluate the value of promotional funds being spent on publicity activities and community programs.

8. Contrast Wendy's promotional approach to the family market through adults with that segment of McDonald's advertising which focuses on children. List advantages and disadvantages of both approaches.

COMMUNICATION APPEALS TO ADULTS	
Advantages	Disadvantages

COMMUNICATION APPEALS TO CHILDREN	
Advantages	Disadvantages

9. Evaluate Wendy's drive-in window as an overall selling point for the restaurant.

_____

_____

_____

_____

_____

_____

_____

_____

_____

10. What other types of research do you think Wendy's should undertake at this point?

_____

_____

_____

_____

_____

_____

_____

274

11. Discuss the relative advantages and disadvantages of print, television, and radio advertising for Wendy's.

MEDIA	ADVANTAGES	DISADVANTAGES
Radio		
Television		
Print		

12. Based on your statement of the problems facing Wendy's as given in question 1 and your analysis of the case, what specific recommendations would you make to Wendy's and why?

Overall Recommendations: _____

_____

_____

_____

_____

Rationale for Recommendations: _____

_____

_____

_____

_____

ANALYSIS FORM

Case 24

Kalsø Systemet, Inc.

1. Based on your analysis of the case and your knowledge of the existing marketing environment what do you see as the present and possible future problems facing Kalsø Systemet?

_____

_____

_____

_____

_____

_____

_____

_____

_____

_____

2. Based on the concentric circles shown here, how would you describe the competition for Earth shoes? Describe each circle as a level of competition moving from the closest (B) to the furthest (E) away from Earth shoes.

A. Earth shoes _____

B. _____

C. _____

D. _____

E. _____

3. Discuss how the five steps in the consumer adoption process might take place as they relate to a consumer "adopting" Earth shoes.

ADOPTION PROCESS	DESCRIPTION OF STEP RELATED TO EARTH SHOES
Awareness	
Interest	
Evaluation	
Trial	
Adoption	

278

4. Present and future adopters of a product like Earth shoes can fall into one of five categories. Offer a brief description of the characteristics of Earth shoe consumers who have or will fall into each of the five categories.

TYPE OF ADOPTER	PROBABLE DESCRIPTION OF THIS ADOPTER OF EARTH SHOES
Innovators	
Early Adopter	
Early Majority	
Late Majority	
Laggards	

5. Discuss some of the possible advertising themes that could be used by Earth shoes.

_____

_____

_____

_____

_____

_____

_____

_____

_____

6. Should advertising for Earth shoes be concentrated at the national, local, or both levels? Why?

_____

_____

_____

_____

_____

_____

_____

_____

_____

_____

_____

7. Discuss the advantages and disadvantages of print, television, and radio advertising for Earth shoes:

TYPE OF MEDIA	ADVANTAGES	DISADVANTAGES
Print		
Television		
Radio		

281

8. Do you evaluate the use of a toll-free telephone number as a good marketing strategy for Earth shoes? Why or why not?

_____

_____

_____

_____

_____

_____

_____

_____

_____

_____

_____

_____

_____

_____

9. Indicate why you feel Earth shoes should or should not use each of the following types of distribution strategy.

DISTRIBUTION STRATEGY	WHY USE OR NOT USE
Intensive	
Selective	
Exclusive	

10. What other types of products would be appropriate for the Earth shoe stores to carry?

_____

_____

_____

_____

_____

_____

_____

_____

11. Discuss any types of marketing research you feel would be appropriate for Kalsø Systemet to undertake at this time.

_____

_____

_____

_____

_____

_____

_____

_____

_____

_____

12. Based on your analysis of the case and consistent with the problem statement you made in question 1 indicate what specific recommendations you would make to Kalsø Systemet. Also indicate your supporting rationale.

Specific Recommendations: _____

_____

_____

_____

_____

Rationale for Recommendations: _____

_____

_____

_____

_____

ANAYLSIS FORM

Case 25

Diversified Information Systems Corporation

1. How would you define the "real business" of DISC?

_____

_____

_____

_____

_____

_____

_____

2. From your evaluation of the case what would you say are the major problems facing DISC at this time?

_____

_____

_____

_____

_____

_____

_____

_____

_____

285

3. Two major market segments for the DISC system are insurance companies and individual insurance agencies. Respond to the following questions about these segments.

QUESTION	INSURANCE COMPANIES	INSURANCE AGENCIES
What are their needs for systems like DISC?		
What are their possible objections against purchase?		
What would be your responses to these objections?		

4. Assume that leasing firms are unwilling to arrange leases to individual insurance agencies for the full $46,900 value of the complete DISC system. Some leasing firms are willing to make lease arrangements for up to $22,000 based on the value of the hardware equipment used in the DISC system. What alternatives are open to DISC in terms of making a sale to an insurance agency under these circumstances?

_____

_____

_____

_____

_____

_____

_____

_____

_____

_____

_____

_____

5. If DISC's out-of-pocket costs for the hardware used in the complete system is $18,000, what would be the potential advantages and disadvantages for DISC itself to carry a second lease with the insurance agency for the difference between the selling price for the complete system and the amount that leasing firms are willing to carry?

Advantages: _____

_____

_____

Disadvantages: _____

_____

_____

6. Describe and discuss possible strategies DISC could use in encouraging potential customers to visit DISC's home office for an on-the-spot demonstration of its system's capabilities.

_____

_____

_____

_____

_____

_____

_____

_____

_____

_____

7. What other industries or lines of business might offer potential markets for software systems similar to those presently offered by DISC?

_____

_____

_____

_____

_____

_____

_____

_____

288

8. What would you use as your four major selling points in communicating with prospective customers about the DISC system?

a. _____

_____

_____

_____

_____

b. _____

_____

_____

_____

_____

c. _____

_____

_____

_____

_____

d. _____

_____

_____

_____

_____

_____

9. From the perspective of communicating with prospective customers for the DISC system, evaluate the following approaches in terms of their advantages and disadvantages for DISC.

APPROACHES	ADVANTAGES	DISADVANTAGES
Booths at professional meetings		
Direct-mail campaigns		
Personal visits to prospective customers		
Personal visits by prospective customers to DISC's home office		
Advertising in insurance journals and magazines		

10. What other types of communication efforts could be used by DISC to reach prospective customers for its system?

_____

_____

_____

_____

_____

_____

_____

_____

_____

11. Based on your evaluation in questions 9 and 10 what specific communications strategy would you recommend for DISC and why?

   Recommended Communication Strategy: _____

_____

_____

_____

   Rationale for These Recommendations: _____

_____

_____

_____

_____

12. Based on your statement of the problems facing DISC (question 2) and your analysis of the case, what specific recommendations would you make to DISC and why?

Overall Recommendations: _____

_____

_____

_____

_____

Rationale for Recommendations: _____

_____

_____

_____

_____

_____

_____

ANALYSIS FORM

Case 26

Volkswagen of America
The Rabbit

1. Discuss how the following environmental factors are impacting upon the atuomotive industry.

Social and Cultural	Legal and Political
Economic	Competitive

2. Discuss the relative importance of the factors which caused Volkswagen
   sales to decrease in the United States.

   _____

   _____

   _____

   _____

   _____

   _____

   _____

   _____

   _____

   _____

   _____

   _____

   _____

3. Indicate how the following concepts might apply to Volkswagen.

   Undifferentiated Marketing: _____

   _____

   _____

   Market Segmentation: _____

   _____

   _____

   Concentrated Marketing: _____

   _____

   _____

294

4. In terms of the marketing research results reported in the case, respond to the following:
   a. What are the major conclusions that can be drawn from the data?

   _____

   _____

   _____

   _____

   _____

   _____

   _____

   _____

   b. What other types of analyses should be done on the existing data?

   _____

   _____

   _____

   _____

   _____

   _____

   _____

   _____

   _____

   _____

c. What other types of marketing research should be gathered?

_____

_____

_____

_____

_____

_____

_____

_____

_____

_____

d. How would you recommend that these data be gathered?

_____

_____

_____

_____

_____

_____

_____

_____

_____

_____

_____

5. Based on the information in the case what do you see as the basic marketing strengths and weaknesses of the Rabbit?

Strengths: _____

_____

_____

_____

_____

Weaknesses: _____

_____

_____

_____

_____

6. Discuss the strategy of market segmentation as you would use it to market the Rabbit.

_____

_____

_____

_____

_____

_____

_____

_____

_____

_____

_____

7. Relate how the concept of lifestyle could be utilized in the marketing of the Rabbit.

_____

_____

_____

_____

_____

_____

_____

_____

_____

_____

_____

_____

8. Discuss the importance of the concept of cognitive dissonance as it may relate to the purchase of a Rabbit.

_____

_____

_____

_____

_____

_____

_____

9. Indicate how you would utilize each of the following elements in developing the promotional mix for the Rabbit.

ELEMENT	USE IN PROMOTIONAL MIX FOR RABBIT
Advertising	
Personal Selling	
Sales Promotion	
Public Relations Publicity	

299

10. Based on your overall evaluation of the case, what specific recommendations would you give to Volkswagen regarding the Rabbit?

_____

_____

_____

_____

_____

_____

_____

_____

_____

_____

_____

_____

_____

_____